BIBLE for VITAL Congregations

BIBLE
for VITAL
Congregations

Barbara J. Essex

Anthony B. Robinson, Series Editor

THE
PILGRIM
PRESS
Cleveland

The Pilgrim Press, 700 Prospect Avenue East,
Cleveland, Ohio 44115-1100
thepilgrimpress.com
©2008 by The Pilgrim Press

Biblical quotations are from the *New Revised Standard Version of the Bible*, ©1989 by the Division of Christian Education of the National Council of Churches of Christ in the U.S.A., and are used by permission.

 Printed in the United States of America on acid-free paper that contains 30% post-consumer fiber.

Library of Congress Cataloging-in-Publication Data

Essex, Barbara J. (Barbara Jean), 1951—
Bible for vital congregations / Barbara J. Essex.
p. cm. — (Congregational vitality series)
Includes bibliographical references.
ISBN 13: 978-0-8298-1732-4 (alk. paper)
1. Bible—Introductions. I. Title.
BS475.3.E87 2008
220.6'1 — dc22

2007045690

Contents

Foreword

With respect to the Bible, those of us involved in the Congregational Vitality Initiative are convinced of two things: there are no vital Christian congregations without Scripture/Bible, and many churches and Christians have tried for too long to get by without a lively and loving relationship with God's message to us in the Bible. Barbara Essex is just the person to help congregations, clergy and ordinary Christians remedy this situation.

Barbara is a teacher and student of the Bible who has brought its stories to life in a series of best-selling books published by The Pilgrim Press. Here, Barbara takes on an awe-inspiring task: introducing the whole Bible and making it accessible and engaging for beginners.

Barbara begins with the story of her own journey with the Scriptures. She didn't know the Bible well herself when she encountered one of the church's great preachers and teachers, Dr. Jeremiah Wright. Wright's sermons intrigued Barbara with the Bible's stories and provoked her with a challenge. Wright said *all* Christians need to know the Bible. Barbara tells us how the Bible touched and changed her life.

Building on this personal story and testimony, Barbara invites her readers on a journey of understanding and delight that is the balance of the book. She helps us understand Bible study and the tools it requires. She provides a helpful overview of the entire Biblical story—that is, Barbara helps us to get a glimpse of the forest before we descend into the trees for a closer look. So often readers of the Bible lack that sense of the overall narrative and do get lost in the forest, a forest that can be pretty dense and dark at times when we become tangled in the thickets of Leviticus or turn in circles in Romans!

As the journey continues, Barbara invites a deeper engagement with a series of key texts and stories from different parts of the Biblical canon. In doing so, she manages a smorgasbord that is not just filling, but also nourishing.

I hope that many congregations, adult study groups, classes, and individuals will pick up this book in one hand and their Bible in the other and prepare for the adventure of a lifetime. I hope that with both books in hand we will enter into group study and discussions, because the Bible really comes alive in the context of the community of faith—the community of faith, not solitary individual study, is the native habitat of the Bible. And I hope that, after studying and using Barbara's wonderful book, our experience of worship will be deepened by a fresh sense of the gift and power of Scripture.

In every great renewal movement in the church—Josiah's reforms in the seventh century BCE in Israel, Jesus and the early church in the first century, the Reformation in the sixteenth century and Vatican II in the twentieth century—a rediscovery of the Bible has been at the heart of new life. Moreover, in these powerful movements and moments, the Bible has been reclaimed not as a book of rules, but as a book and message of life with the power to change lives and change the world. May it be so among us today!

Anthony B. Robinson
General Editor, Congregational Vitality Initiative Book Series

Preface

A basic book about the Bible...what a concept! I've already written several volumes of Bible study resources: among others, *Bad Girls of the Bible: Exploring Women of Questionable Virtue* (The Pilgrim Press: Cleveland, 1999), *Bad Boys of the Bible: Exploring Men of Questionable Virtue* (The Pilgrim Press: Cleveland, 2002), *Krazy Kinfolk: Exploring Dysfunctional Families of the Bible* (The Pilgrim Press: Cleveland, 2005), and *Misbehavin' Monarchs: Exploring Biblical Monarchs of Questionable Character* (The Pilgrim Press: Cleveland, 2006). My mission is to make the Bible accessible and fun and I have enjoyed some success in this endeavor. So I was pleased when Anthony Robinson asked me to write a short book on Bible for Vital Congregations for the UCC's Congregational Vitality Initiative.

I understand the concern that haunts many church leaders—while members of our congregations are more educated than ever, they continue to know less and less about the Bible. Pastors bemoan the lack of interest in Bible study despite the popularity of fictionalized versions of the biblical message that make tons of money for authors and filmmakers. It seems that the popular renditions of the Bible and its various stories do not compel people to search the scripture for themselves.

Whenever I preach, listeners are quick to praise if I, in their words, "make the Bible understandable for them." They are amazed and fascinated by the backstory of biblical texts—some say they never really understood the biblical story, despite being in the church their whole lives.

Seminary students are often disoriented when they learn the "real" story of the Bible—the various perspectives, the diversity of source materials, the uncertainty of what we know. They feel that their faith is undermined when they dissect the motivations for the writings and how the works have been used in public discourse. Many Christians have a disdain for the Bible—they have been hurt by the interpretation of its message. Or they are frustrated as they attempt to read it and make sense of the biblical story. Or they question the relevancy of an ancient book for contemporary life.

The challenge is to figure out where to start—how does one begin the work of reading the Bible? There are thousands of volumes related to the Bible and biblical study. Some of them are quite technical and written for academic settings. Others are simplified but lack depth or ignore the complexities of the Bible.

It is easy to see how overwhelming the enterprise of studying the Bible can be.

So, I propose we start at the beginning by asking some fundamental questions—what is the Bible? How did it come to be? How can we read it? What authority does it have for us today? What tools do we need to help our understanding? Why should we bother?

I am grateful to Tony Robinson for the invitation to try to answer these questions. His support and encouragement have been invaluable, as I have waded through the immense information available to us about the Bible. I've had to keep reminding myself that I am not writing a comprehensive commentary or in-depth study of the Bible—my task is to get you thinking about the Bible enough to pick it up and begin your own conversation with the book that shapes and supports our faith. In other words, I've kept telling myself to "keep it simple" without making this work simplistic. We will see if I lived up to the challenge.

In addition to Tony Robinson, general editor for the CVI series, I am ever thankful to the folks at Pilgrim Press, especially Kim Martin Sadler, whose support remains unconditional and strong. A special thank you to José Malayang and the Local Church Ministries Covenanted Ministry team of the United Church of Christ for the vision that led to this initiative. Any strength of this volume is due to input from all who challenged and critiqued my thinking and research. All weaknesses are due to my own inadequacies.

Please note that three conventions which are widely accepted in biblical study and analysis are used in this book. (1) The first portion of the Bible is referred to as the "Hebrew Bible" rather than Old Testament, except for explanatory purposes. The Hebrew Bible is a collection preserved by the Jewish community, and this is their name for that collection. (2) Dates are noted as BCE (Before the Common Era) rather than BC (Before Christ) and CE (Common Era) rather than AD (*Anno Domini* or "in the year of the Lord"). The older labels show a bias toward the Christian view of scripture which the newer designations avoid. (3) The God who reveals the divine identity to Moses is designated by YHWH—the tetragrammaton for the Hebrew name. This name for God is so holy that Jews do not speak it; English Bibles typically translate YHWH as "the LORD."

Introduction

Walk into almost any bookstore and you will find shelves lined with Bibles —student editions, large print editions, contemporary language editions, red-letter editions, gender-specific editions, occupation-specific editions, age-specific editions. The Bible enjoys a longstanding spot on top of the bestsellers' list. It is the beloved book of Christians the world over. Yet no book has caused as much controversy as the Bible. We hear that many Christians are biblically illiterate—intimidated and unfamiliar with the book that helps to shape their faith and that governs their understanding of the world. The Bible is used to oppress various groups of persons. It is used as a tool for revolutionary work that is sometimes violent. And it is used as a way of escaping social responsibility and accountability. The Bible is many things to many people—some of those things are positive and life-giving, but some are damaging and life-denying.

Pick up a Bible, any Bible, and try to read it—there are unfamiliar names of people and places from far away, both in time and distance. There are concepts that mean one thing in a secular setting and something entirely different in a religious one. There are ideas that convey different understandings in different time periods. There are a multitude of images and metaphors used to describe God and God's relationships with God's people. There are lists of names and places, some of which scholars have been unable to identify or locate. There are complicated timelines that seem to contradict themselves and confuse even the most conscientious reader. Some stories are repeated verbatim, while others appear similar but with differences that are difficult to account for, even for those whose life's work is the study of the Bible. There are various traditions interwoven within the Bible—some are smoothly integrated, while others leave us with questions about the who, what, where, why and how of people, places, things, and ideas.

There are historical events that should be straightforward—either the events happened or they didn't. Right? Well, not exactly. Different communities remember some events in different time periods, and they are remembered within the social, political, and theological context of the one telling the story. There are questions about whether some events actually happened at all—are they metaphors for some theological point of the biblical writer or that writer's community?

With so much diversity within and controversy about the Bible, what can we know for sure? Can we know anything about the Bible with absolute certainty? If you are wrestling with these and other questions about the Bible, you are not alone. In fact, you belong to a special club that has been wrestling with this book for centuries. Many of us wonder just what this Bible is and why we should care about it at all.

Bible for Vital Congregations is a volume designed to give you an understandable and accessible overview of the Bible and its relevance for the church today. Here, we hope to untangle some of the threads of the Bible and lay out a foundation from which to read, study, and understand this powerful work that forms and informs our Christian faith and tradition. This is a journey into a world that is very different from our own—but, in so many ways, it is a world too much like our own. In fact, the words that were spoken by, to, and for folks over two thousand years ago are words that we need to hear even in the twenty-first century.

The first "problem" with the Bible is that it is not any *one* thing. It would be great if the Bible were just a narrative tracing one family's journey. It would be helpful if the Bible were just a book of poetry with images and symbols that are apparent. It would be logical if the Bible were a book of historical events, told by one narrator from one point of view. It would be wonderful if the Bible were an expanded list of concepts about God and humanity. It would even help if the Bible were a list of do's and don'ts for everyday life. Instead, the Bible is all these things—and more!

Some scholars suggest that we should approach the Bible first as a drama—a work of literature that has a beginning, a middle and an ending; a work that has a plot that moves towards a climax; a work that has a cast of interesting characters—both major and minor; a work that has a conflict that is resolved by its end. There is something to be said for taking this approach, for the Bible is like a drama in many ways. What separates the Bible from a good novel or play, however, is its cast of characters. The main character of the Bible is God! What is even more remarkable is that God is actively involved in human affairs—God is author and director in charge of casting the various roles, outlining the action, determining set designs, and making sure the scenes are effective. Not only that, in this drama God has an agenda, a purpose for the action. In this drama, we must pay attention to so much—plot, character development, conflict and conflict resolution, dialogue, motivation, and outcomes.

So we have our work cut out for us. We are working within the limitations of this short overview. Our task is to explore some basics about the Bible—what it is, how it came to be, how we can study it, why it is important, why we use it, and where it will take us.

Every written document comes with a set of assumptions and points towards a particular purpose. This volume is no different. We will be working with some fundamental assumptions. It is assumed that *Bible for Vital Congregations* will be read alongside the Bible by Christians of the Reformed tradition; will serve as a study guide for teaching and preaching the Bible; and will be understood as an introduction to further study. For some, this book is a refresher course in Bible basics; for others, it will be the first step in serious study of the Bible. Whether you are a seasoned student of the Bible or a newcomer to its riches, it is our hope that this small volume will be of practical use.

The Bible is our book, the book of and about our faith—it is the story about God and God's dealings with us. It is a book that we approach through and with faith, but this does not mean that we cannot ask critical questions— we must. And we must understand that such inquiry does not diminish our faith; rather, it deepens our faith by compelling us to plumb its depths for meaning and direction. It is through studying the Bible that we get glimpses of who God is, who we are, and the ways in which we belong to and resist God. It is through studying the Bible that we begin to understand God's vision and purpose for creation—one of love, peace, harmony, unity, power and community. It is through the Bible that we encounter a God who professes unconditional love for us and a Christ who beckons us to follow him. The Bible is the foundation for our worship—we base our liturgies, hymns, prayers and sermons on the words that we know to be God's Word. God's vision, through the biblical witness, is an answer to what ails so many of us. While we suffer with anxiety, alienation, greed, and isolation, God envisions and invites us into a world of life, joy, community, and wholeness. The Bible assures us and reassures us that we are not alone in the world—that we are in partnership with the One who was, is now, and will forever be—God with us!

One

The Bible, Faith, and Me

It may seem strange to begin a book about the Bible with a personal testimony. Then again, it is not that strange. The Bible itself is a testimony—a series of testimonies about the power and presence of God in the world and in the lives of ancient people. One of the more remarkable things we can say about the Bible is that it still speaks to us—thousands of years after its beginnings. And the Bible still speaks to me in powerful, life-giving, and life-changing ways.

I have always loved to read. There are few things more rewarding than being swept up by a good story. I've spent countless hours digging into novels, short stories, poems, and even comic books. Reading was always fun and it continues to be one of my favorite pastimes. But it never occurred to me to read the Bible! Our family Bible was huge and sat on the coffee table, mostly gathering dust. I remember my mother filling in the blanks on pages that recorded one's family tree. But I don't recall anyone actually reading it. In fact, that Bible was sacred and the only time we were allowed to touch it was when we dusted. Despite its place of prominence on the living room table, it was not a book for handling. I took for granted that the Bible was a hands-off book in our home. I didn't sneak to touch or read it—it was special and that was that.

I joined the church the summer of my thirteenth birthday during a revival at my maternal grandmother's church in Birmingham, Alabama. In that revival service I felt something—the preacher was so skillful at storytelling that I expected to see Jesus walk through the church doors. I asked my grandmother if I could join the church; she asked why. I confessed a faith that God was real and that Jesus was alive in my heart and in my life. And it was true—during the preaching, I felt something I had never felt before—a connection to something, someone beyond myself. It was a powerful experience and I was hungry for more. I began reading the Bible—not the big Bible on the coffee table, but a small King James Version that I had received as a gift. But I was quickly turned off—the language was just too strange. Although I was a good reader and did well in English, I couldn't quite get the rhythm of the Bible—there were just too many words that didn't reflect the way I talked. Imagine how my friends would have reacted had I spoken the way they did in the Bible—"verily, verily, I saith unto thee…" I don't think the Chicago Southside folks I knew would have invited me to join them for anything!

Language was not the only stumbling block for me regarding the Bible. The story didn't make much sense. I couldn't make connections—it seemed that the Bible was an anthology of unrelated parts. I didn't see the connection between creation and the words of the prophets. The Psalms were good poetry, but Proverbs was a mystery. The Gospels were pretty easy to follow, but the Epistles seemed incomplete—and don't even get me started about the Book of Revelation!

The preaching I heard while growing up also left me baffled. Except for that one revivalist, most preachers left me confused about the Bible story and its relevance for my life. It was frustrating, and boring, to sit through long sermons and get nothing from them.

I attended Sunday school for a time. The lessons were either simplistic or boring—despite the efforts of good-hearted, well-intentioned teachers, the lessons did not engage me. I didn't feel anything, although I desperately wanted to relive the experience of my conversion. But my ongoing spiritual quest was dry and lifeless. There were still moments when sermons and lessons were meaningful, but they were increasingly episodic—I was not consistently nurtured or challenged. I soon dropped out of the church because I thought something was wrong with me—others seemed to love church and seemed to enjoy the worship services. I felt that something was missing and it was my fault that I wasn't getting it.

It wasn't until my mid-twenties that I ventured back to church in a real way. I was shopping for a church that would help revitalize my faith, and I found it. I first visited Trinity United Church of Christ (Chicago) as a favor for a friend, a member who had invited me many times to join her in worship. I had never heard of the United Church of Christ and was curious. My friend wasn't able to give me much background about the UCC; I knew about several branches of the Baptist church and my mother had been a member of an African Methodist Episcopal Church—but what was this UCC? But I trusted my friend and I decided to risk attending a worship service with her. I was searching for some kind of spiritual nurture.

When I heard Jeremiah A. Wright, Jr., preach, I was transported back to that little Baptist church in Birmingham—I felt something in the message. His preaching was clear, vibrant, moving—just like the preaching of that revivalist in Birmingham. Dr. Wright's sermon was a perfect balance of teaching and inspiration. He talked about what the text meant to its original listeners and what the message can mean for us. I was fascinated with the biblical characters of the text and how God used them, and how God wants to use us. I even took notes on the sermon—I wrote down questions the sermon raised for me and I wrote down things I wanted to remember. The sermon was a learning experience—just what I was looking for. But that was not enough.

Sunday after Sunday, Dr. Wright would admonish "so-called" Christians who didn't know the Bible—and whenever he went on this tirade, it was as if he were looking right at me! My guilt about being biblically illiterate was getting to me. So I started going to one of the weekly Bible studies at the church. It was a real class. We had a textbook and homework assignments, and we were encouraged to ask questions. Even more amazing, we were encouraged to read and write in our Bibles! The Bible was no longer an untouchable volume—it became a real book. I found myself asking God and Jesus questions as I read. The resources we used—commentaries, atlases, and concordances—opened up the biblical texts in ways that made them come alive. I was energized by my study and the discussions we had about the texts were invigorating—nothing was off limits. We were encouraged to approach the Bible from our particular contexts—I could read the Bible as a woman, an African American, an educated person…and find myself in the message. It was empowering to search for myself in the stories, to put myself in the stories, and to imagine myself engaging the characters in my contemporary setting.

When I answered the call to ordained ministry, I was both confronted and challenged by a passage, Isaiah 41:9–10:

> You whom I took from the ends of the earth,
> and called from its farthest corners,

saying to you, "You are my servant,
I have chosen you and not cast you off";
do not fear, for I am with you,
do not be afraid, for I am your God;
I will strengthen you, I will help you,
I will uphold you with my victorious right hand.

You should know that I was reluctant to answer God's call into ministry. There were no ministers in my immediate or extended family. The women in ministry whom I knew worked secular jobs because churches didn't want to call women as pastors. I had a job that paid well and I had heard that ministers didn't make much money. And beyond that, I didn't want to be a minister. I didn't feel that I was good enough. I felt I lacked the "holiness factor" in that my prayer life was inconsistent, I hadn't paid dues by serving in other church capacities—I had not been an usher, I had not taught Sunday School, I had not sung in the choir. I felt that God was picking on me. I wasn't ready or qualified to be a minister.

In the midst of all my doubts and questions and insecurities, I was led to this text in Isaiah. It is a passage I have returned to time and time again. It speaks to me about God's desire to use me in the service of God's intentions for creation, and assures me that I am not alone in this adventure of service. Whenever I am frustrated or fearful about the work God has entrusted in me, I refer back to these words in Isaiah and I am fortified for the work ahead of me. The Bible reminds me that I stand in a legacy of humans—flawed and frail in so many ways—ordinary women and men who do their best for God, out of gratitude for God's tender mercies and power.

I was so hyped by the Bible, I wanted to share that excitement with others. My seminary experience opened up new dimensions of the Bible—looking critically at the Bible has not diluted or dampened my faith. Instead, my faith is deepened and strengthened by critically engaging the texts. I couldn't wait to share my new learnings with others. I started teaching Bible study classes at Trinity and soon had many students—some, I'm sure, were curious about a woman teaching the Bible (remember this was in the early 1980s when women were just entering the ministry in substantial numbers); most, I hope, were more curious about the Bible itself. We had quite a time—so many questions, so many doubts, so many ways to approach the Bible. Well, there was never a dull moment in those classes. I was driven by my own thirst for God's Word and challenged by my students whose questions were always fresh and intriguing. When I became a pastor, my love for the Bible deepened. I needed the Bible to help members understand the faith we claim, to help us deal with uncomfortable issues and situations, to help us make it through the trials and tribulations of living from day to day.

After 25 years of studying, preaching and teaching, I am still amazed by the Bible. No matter how many times I read a passage, I still am confronted by something new. I still encounter God and Jesus on its pages. I still get swept up in the drama and action of the Bible. I can feel Noah's bewildered response to God's command to build an ark when there was no cloud in the sky. I sit with Hagar as she weeps and wails in the wilderness over her child whose life hangs in the balance after they have been put out of Abraham's house. I can hear Moses' objections to God's call to deliver God's people out of slavery in Africa—why me? I get glimpses of Saul as he hides in the baggage room to avoid becoming the ruler of Israel. I can see Ezekiel standing at the makeshift grave of dry bones, in despair because there was no logical way for those bones to ever live again. I can feel the eyes of Jesus as he looks upon those who are sick, alienated, hopeless. I can hear the laughter of joy as Miriam sings and dances on the shores of the Sea of Reeds—the Red Sea. I am moved by Mary who pours the last of her expensive perfume on Jesus' feet. I can hear the moans of those who witness Jesus hanging on that rugged cross as his blood oozes from his wrists—I was there when they crucified my Savior.

These and other images are imprinted on my heart and spirit, and I can recall them by simply picking up the Bible. The Bible always has a word for me—a word of comfort, a word of assurance, a word of liberation, a word that pushes me to consider the new thing that God continues to do in the world. No matter what I am going through, there is always a word, just for me. I am assured by reading the Bible that I am never alone—that God's presence is constant and consistent; that Jesus empathizes with me in every situation and condition; that I am part of a family not defined by its dysfunctions of "–isms" (racism, sexism, ageism, able-ism, militarism, etc.); that I am invited to dream a world that is not limited by grief, doubt, or shadows.

Through the Bible, God calls me to be better and to do better—not from a works righteous or perfectionist way, but out of gratitude to a God who is better to me than I can ever be to myself. Through the preaching and teaching of the church, I am nudged to release grudges and judgments about others, to look beyond the surface to see kinship with those who are not like me, to let my guard down to risk connecting with others, to keep my ego in check, to grow. The Bible helps me to see something other than what I experience.

I love the Bible. And I pray that you will grow to love it, too. I hope my personal testimony whets your appetite to delve into this book that helps to shape our faith and our faith communities. I hope that you will venture into the pages of this book that points to a God who does marvelous things, not because we are good or deserve them, but because God is faithful, gracious, and compassionate. The Bible is a gift and what a gift we have—thanks be to God!

Reflection Questions

1. What do you hope to gain by studying the Bible?

2. How is your faith informed or shaped by the Bible?

3. What do you bring to the Bible that will determine or shape how you read the texts?

Two

The Bible: Read All About It

People of the Book" is a phrase that describes Jews, Christians, and **Muslims. But we aren't talking about just any old book—we are talking about *the* book about God.** And I'm sure your next question is: what makes it *the* book about God? Aren't there other books about God, too? Should we consider those books as foundational, too? These are good questions, and religious leaders of each of these faith traditions asked the same questions. The Bible has shaped each of these world religions because they share a common ancestry—Abraham, the founder of belief in one god—as their catalyst.

What's more, the Bible has found its way into our secular life—in fact, the Bible informs the Declaration of Independence, the Constitution, and various civil laws that define and shape our national identity and common life. Even in local contexts, we often quote and misquote biblical passages—in matters of justice, we say, "an eye for an eye;" in matters of civility, we say, "turn the other cheek;" in matters of community life, we say, "do unto others as we would have them do unto us."

Not only that, the Bible has influenced art, music, and literature. Many of the great hymns of the church are biblically-based. The stained glass windows of our churches depict characters and scenes from the Bible. During worship services we recite passages of scripture in the call to worship, in the prayers, in the benediction, and in other elements of congregational life. We find references to the Bible in the writings of authors as diverse as William Shakespeare and Toni Morrison. In fact, some of what we know about the Bible is because of John Milton's *Paradise Lost* and popular films like "The Ten Commandments." Biblical issues, obvious or not, underlie all sorts of films—"Go Tell It on the Mountain," "The End of the Affair," "The Apostle," "Leap of Faith," "Saved!," "Dogma," "The Mission," "Beloved," "The Color Purple," "Matrix," and on and on.

We would be hard pressed to take the Bible out of our personal and social lives—it's everywhere. But that fact still doesn't help us understand why the Bible is so important.

Why Study the Bible?

The Bible is "scripture" for Christians—the revealed Word of God inspired by the Holy Spirit to men and women. The Bible is a collection of works that keep alive the memory of God's saving acts in the world. From Genesis to Revelation, the Bible is about God and God's dealings with us. The Bible is a reliable and normative witness to who God is and what God does and will do. As scripture, the Bible is authoritative for our faith and community. The Bible, as our sacred text, points us to God who gives, sustains, challenges, and nurtures our faith and our community. The Bible shows us a God who is reliable and trustworthy, even in difficult times and situations. By studying the Bible, we learn who we are and what we should be doing.

The Bible, as God's Word, challenges and confronts us on many levels. We should not be the same once we start to dig into the Bible's riches. We turn to the Bible to learn about the nature and purposes of God and to learn what God expects of us—to push beyond our comfort zones. In the Bible, we encounter God, Jesus Christ, and the Holy Spirit. The Bible provides a word of comfort for rough times but also provides a word that challenges us to work with God to create a world marked by justice, peace, and love. The Bible energizes us to dream a world governed by values that create community. Through reading and studying the Bible, we are empowered to engage in ministry and mission. Power—there is power in the Bible and it's available for us. Transformation—there is transformation available for us when we actively engage the Bible. Life—there is life for us in the Bible. Courage—there is courage offered when we diligently study the Bible. Hope—there is hope in the Bible for this present age and for the ages to come.

The Bible informs our understandings, confessions, and statements about who we are and whose we are, from the beginning of time and beyond time. The Bible is not just about the way things were back in the day. It points to a living God who continues to guide and challenge us, who gives life and transforms us and the world through divine grace, mercy, and compassion. The Bible also points to a God who chastises and challenges us to do more and to be better people. Jesus of Nazareth is a disturbing figure—we feel we can approach him as a safe companion, but Jesus forces us to question the assumptions that we take for granted. His sermons and questions pierce us at the very core of our being and we are forced to make decisions that are not always easy. The choices that Jesus made during his time on earth push us to consider our own choices and we often feel inadequate. The Bible assures us that we have all we need to be God's hands and feet—we already have the confidence, power, skills, and will to do what makes for community.

As you can imagine, there were a lot of people who wanted to make their experiences and understandings the norm and standard by which others judged their faithfulness to God. It is human nature to make one's experience the norm. But with so much diversity, there had to be some common understandings about what was authoritative and authentic and what was not. This challenge led to the process of canonization. "Canon" (from a Greek word that means "rule" or "standard") is the term used to identify the list of official sacred writings of Judaism and Christianity—that is, the canon determines what writings we consider to be scripture.

The process of setting the canon was a long one and the details are obscure and fuzzy. There is no doubt that a great variety of material—oral and written—circulated during the formative days of Judaism and later, the formative days of Christianity. We know that a multitude of perspectives, opinions, and understandings abounded. The task of synagogue and church leaders was to determine what writings were authoritative and should be used during congregational gatherings, preaching and teaching, and personal study, without worrying about whether the texts strayed from the common understanding of the faith.

The canon, as we have it today, is itself a reflection of that great diversity of thought—even a superficial reading of the Bible shows that it is a diverse and varied work. We know some voices were left out—which ones and why? We don't have many answers to these questions. What we know is that the process of setting the canon was the result of a long historical process. One test was to determine what religious concepts and rituals connected religious communities. What did these communities hold in common? That is, what could be agreed upon about the faith? This is the work of canon and authority —it is theological work with a concern for a common and shared life.

With so many voices vying for legitimacy, who would determine what writings were to be authoritative for all members of the faith? Was there a baseline from which all communities connected to the faith should act? These questions only generate more questions: who determined what was sacred? On what basis was the determination made? What made a text reliable and credible? What happened to the voices that are not included? So many questions, so few definitive answers.

Scholars think that certain writings were designated authoritative based on their use in various religious communities—the use of the writings determined what was judged to be true teaching. Respected church leaders had a hand in setting the canon—leaders who were themselves judged reliable and trustworthy. These leaders had the awe-inspiring task of determining which texts were more foundational, inspirational, edifying, and so on. The important thing to know is that the canonization process did not happen in a vacuum; it happened in the community of the faithful as they wrestled with what constituted true faith and what oral and written materials supported the faith.

And if you think the Christian community had an easier time setting its canon—think again! Remember that Christianity's roots are in Judaism— Jesus was Jewish, not Christian. When Jesus spoke of the "scriptures," he meant what we now call the Hebrew Bible—the Torah, the Prophets, and the Writings. And to muddy the waters even more, there were all kinds of materials being used in Christian churches and gatherings that tried to explain the Christ event.

We know that Paul and Peter and others were respected leaders—but there were others who also were charismatic, logical, and persuasive. Even the churches founded by Paul were swayed by other teachers (he often admonished them to remember the faith and not go with new teachings). As Christianity evolved, there came to be a felt need to determine what writings would set the norm for Christian faith and life—which works were true, which were fictional? What works were to be used in congregational settings and for personal study? What writings were to be used to set church doctrine and formulate faith creeds?

Eventually church councils were convened to settle the matter. Shortly after 400 CE, a list of sacred writings that form our Christian canon—Old and New Testaments—was developed. There were ongoing challenges to this list and it was not finally fixed until the Reformation—the Council of Trent in 1546 set the Old Testament canon at thirty-nine books (Roman Catholic and Orthodox churches have more) and the New Testament canon with a list of twenty-seven books upon which Roman Catholic, Orthodox and Protestant churches agree.

Some questions about the canon cannot be answered and some continue to be controversial. Contemporary biblical scholarship merely affirms what we already know—the Bible is the product of a small group of people in the ancient Near East (Israel) and a religious minority in the Greco-Roman world (the early church). What we are left with, finally, is a body of work that testifies to a God who cares about us and is active in our history, a Christ who shows us the way to God and how to live in community, and a Holy Spirit that continues to sustain, challenge, and transform us on our journey to fully become God's people.

The Bible is the church's book and functions as the norm for church life and Christian doctrine and understandings. There is much we hold in common and these understandings are evident in our various creeds and statements of faith. The UCC Statement of Faith (as adapted by Robert V. Moss, found on the United Church of Christ website, www.ucc.org/faith.htm#MOSS) rehearses well the biblical foundations of our faith and life together:

> We believe in God, the Eternal Spirit, who is made known to us in Jesus our brother, and to whose deeds we testify:
> God calls the worlds into being, creates humankind in the divine image, and sets before us the ways of life and death.
> God seeks in holy love to save all people from aimlessness and sin.
> God judges all humanity and all nations by that will of righteousness declared through prophets and apostles.
> In Jesus Christ, the man of Nazareth, our crucified and risen Lord, God has come to us and shared our common lot, conquering sin and death and reconciling the whole creation to its Creator.
> God bestows upon us the Holy Spirit, creating and renewing the church of Jesus Christ, binding in covenant faithful people of all ages, tongues, and races.

God calls us into the church to accept the cost and joy of discipleship, to be servants in the service of the whole human family, to proclaim the gospel to all the world and resist the powers of evil, to share in Christ's baptism and eat at his table, to join him in his passion and victory.

God promises to all who trust in the gospel forgiveness of sins and fullness of grace, courage in the struggle for justice and peace, the presence of the Holy Spirit in trial and rejoicing, and eternal life in that kingdom which has no end.

Blessing and honor, glory and power be unto God.

Amen.

The miracle of the Bible is that it is not any *one* thing. It continues to challenge us—we must do the work of interpreting its message for our time in history, our diverse contexts, and the issues that concern us. The stories of our religious ancestors still offer us hope, encouragement, inspiration, and direction. The Bible is the important witness to what it means to be God's people in this age and we continue this witness in our preaching and teaching.

How to Study the Bible?

Whew—so how are you feeling right now? Don't give up or throw in the towel just yet. We are getting to the good stuff, and good stuff it is. But where to start? That's a good question. The first thing you will notice is that the Bible is a long story—many Bibles are over a thousand pages long—with double columns of text on silky thin paper. So, how does one go about reading and studying the Bible? Should one start with Genesis and read right through to Revelation? Should one study alone or in a group? Well, again, you have some choices!

How you read and study the Bible will depend on what you want from the experience. Some people do well studying on their own; others want a conversation partner; still others thrive with group study. I find that some combination of all three can help. For most, some devotional time with the Bible will be meaningful. But also, it helps to have the perspectives and viewpoints of others as you make your way through the Bible. The important thing is to have a plan!

The choices continue—do you want to study the Bible book by book, chapter by chapter? Do you want to study the Bible according to themes? Do you want to study the Bible by looking at personalities or events? Do you start with the Gospels and move from there? It's really up to you.

When I served as pastor of a small urban congregation, I found my members were embarrassed about how little they actually knew about the Bible. So we started with a class that dealt with the basics of the Bible; in fact, we borrowed the course name from one taught at Trinity United Church of Christ, "Bible Basics." Each member was encouraged to purchase or borrow a Bible that she was comfortable with and felt good about reading. We spent about four weeks handling the book, browsing through the pages, noting how the Bible is organized, and talking about what made sense and what didn't. At the end of our time, we had a general view of the Bible. Everyone, seasoned Bible readers and those new to it, were on the same page, so to speak. With that solid foundation, we were ready to branch out with our study.

Once everyone was comfortable with the Bible itself, we dug in to explore some of the stories in depth. We decided to look at some themes of the Bible—creation, justice, redemption, salvation, love, mercy, grace. By using concordances and Bible dictionaries, we found sections of the Bible that focused on the themes we wanted to study. Members took turns being responsible for starting the conversation—they brought background information and a set of questions for the class to consider.

Another strategy is to study the Bible according to the lectionary readings each week. I especially enjoyed the lectionary study—members were excited about hearing a sermon based on what they had studied the week before. They felt more connected to the worship because they were able to see how the different elements of worship fit together and their worship deepened their understanding of the Bible.

Yet another strategy is to use specific books designed for Bible study—my own series (*Bad Girls, Bad Boys, Krazy Kinfolk, Misbehavin' Monarchs*) offers examples of stand-alone Bible study books. There are a great number of books on the market—visit a bookstore and spend some time browsing the titles and tables of contents to see what may speak to you. The titles and focus of these books might center on themes, personalities, character traits, particular events, particular words, or some aspect of church doctrine.

In addition to the stand-alone or self-contained Bible studies, there are books tied to the church year. So there are books for study during Advent, Lent, Pentecost, and so on. The bottom line is that there will never be a shortage of materials to help you study the Bible.

With so many choices, you should have a great time exploring the Bible. The important thing is to get started.

Which Bible to Study?

Choosing a Bible is part of the fun! Don't be intimidated by the number of Bibles on bookstore shelves—and there are plenty. I recommend that you carve out some time to check them out. Pick one that makes you feel comfortable. I list some of the more popular ones in the next section, but nothing beats actually holding and skimming Bibles for yourself. Take your time and take it all in. The covers will vary—paper, leather, hardback; some are colorful—pink, black, brown; some are geared for specific audiences—men, women, teenagers, youth, children, mothers, corporate workers. You could spend several days just perusing all the different Bibles, so take your time. You may want to buy more than one; it is good to consult more than one translation. But you may want to have one Bible as your primary study Bible.

I like Bibles with wide margins. I remember sitting in my first Bible study class as a student; my pastor told us to write a phrase in the margin of our Bibles. I was taken aback at first; I had been taught that the Bible was holy and sacred—I couldn't write in it as if it were just any book. But when I took the plunge—believe me, this was a big deal—and actually wrote in my Bible, I felt something happen. I became a partner in conversation with the story, and it was liberating.

Today, I have several Bibles in different translations, but I use one as my primary study Bible. It is totally marked up; sometimes, I have to consult a "clean" Bible to see what it says! My Bible is crowded with comments, various colors of highlighters, and different colors of ink—I really use my Bible. And when I'm re-reading passages, I discover something new and I have to note that, so there are stars, asterisks, exclamation marks, arrows, check marks, and all kinds of words—"Wow!" "Wait!" "Oh, no!" "I don't believe he did that!" "Oh, yeah!" "Ooh, you're going to get it now!" "This is my experience!" "This reminds me of…!"—and, always, questions: "What does this mean?" "What was she thinking?" "Where is God?" "What's going to happen now?" "Didn't you know better?" "What in my experience resonates with this?"

The Bible should be like a good friend—you will want to spend quality time with it, asking it questions, answering questions it asks of you, interacting with the characters, and, of course, conversing with God, Jesus and the Holy Spirit! Sounds a bit crazy, doesn't it? But when you are engrossed in a story, it's like actually being there. Writing is one way of entering the conversation—don't be shy—God is waiting for your participation. And, always, have fun!

There are various English translations of the Bible. In fact, every Bible we have is a translation. Some are literal translations of the Hebrew, Aramaic and Greek; others are non-literal translations and are easier for modern readers to understand. Non-literal translations, though, often make us forget that we are dealing with ancient texts, and they can lose much of the nuance of the original language. With so many Bibles on the market today and new ones being published daily, it is almost impossible to give a comprehensive or complete listing of them. Here, then, is a short overview of a few:

• **King James Version.** The KJV was first published in 1611. Although some of its translations are tendentious and it is based on texts now known by biblical scholarship to be flawed, the KJV is still beloved by many for its poetic language. The style, though, can be intimidating for some—words and phrases such as "thee," "thou," "cometh," "art," and "begat" are archaic forms that may be problematic. While the language has a poetic ring to it, it can be confusing and misleading for modern readers. Newer editions are targeted to specific audiences; for example, the *African American Jubilee Edition* (American Bible Society: New York, 1999), seeks to bridge some of the gap between seventeenth-century monarchical England and the realities of African-American life in the United States by including supplementary material on African culture, the "Black Church," African-American spirituality, music, and worship.

• **New Revised Standard Version.** The NRSV is the version primarily used in theological circles as well as college and seminary classrooms. It is the first translation to involve the work of Protestant, Catholic, Orthodox Christian and Jewish scholars, which makes it an ecumenical enterprise. The NRSV generally reflects more recent knowledge of text, Hebrew and Greek grammar, and lexicon. The most popular edition of the NRSV is the *New Oxford Annotated Bible* (Oxford University Press: New York, 1991), a study Bible with informative articles. The Society of Biblical Literature has produced a new study Bible based on the NRSV, *The Harper Collins Study Bible* (HarperSanFrancisco: San Francisco, 2006), which is highly respected.

• **The New Jewish Version.** The NJV consists of three volumes: *The Torah: The Five Books of Moses; The Prophets: Nebi'im; and The Writings: Kethubim.* These volumes are fairly balanced translations of the three major divisions of the Hebrew Bible. This translation includes the text in Hebrew along with its English equivalent.

• **The New American Bible**. The NAB was prepared by Catholic scholars. This version is generally accurate in its Hebrew and Greek renderings. It uses Old Greek and Qumran (Dead Sea Scrolls) texts rather than the Latin Vulgate.

• **The Jerusalem Bible.** The JB is an English version of a respected French translation of the Bible often used in Roman Catholic circles. It is a helpful translation for church and study use. This version uses "YHWH" to designate the Israelite divine name, rather than "the LORD" used in most modern Christian translations. The JB includes many helpful footnotes.

• **The New English Bible.** The NEB was the first British translation of the Bible after the KJV was written, and includes somewhat more contemporary biblical scholarship. In many ways, it is a counterpart to the NRSV's Oxford Annotated Bible.

• **The Bible in Today's English Version, or The Good News Bible.** The GNB is not a translation but rather a paraphrase. Lacking the formal English style of many other Bibles, it is written to be easily understood. It is geared toward an audience without extensive formal education or without previous experience in reading the Bible. More often than not, this version glosses over awkward syntax, difficult images and idioms; it is easy to read but misses some of the important complexities and nuances of the texts.

• **The New International Version.** The NIV is the best-selling version today; many bookstores carry more editions of this translation than of other translations. Its style of English is generally conservative and so are its theological interpretation; the NIV is also more evangelical in tone. This translation is well marketed and targeted to specific groups (men, mothers, teens, military personnel, etc.).

There are other Bibles; one that is gaining in popularity is *The Message: The Bible in Contemporary Language* (NavPress: Colorado Springs, 2003) by Eugene H. Peterson, a pastor and former seminary teacher of biblical languages. His is a paraphrase of the Bible along the lines of the GNB, but with a sounder theological base. Peterson's intention is to get people reading and he suggests that *The Message* be read alongside more conventional study Bibles. Peterson's renderings are often moving and have the potential of attracting a wide range of readers.

This sampling highlights the reality that there is a variety of Bibles on the market—there is a Bible for anyone and everyone. We encourage you to explore them all and find one or two that work best for your purposes. We don't endorse any particular version; all have some worth and value. For this study, however, we will refer to the NRSV and will supply Hebrew or Greek words where they open up the meaning of the texts. There are Bibles available—read them and experience the joy of eavesdropping on a conversation between God and God's people, ancient and contemporary.

What Tools Are Needed to Study the Bible?

I remember once trying to install a curtain rod in my living room and having a very difficult time of it. When my brother stopped by, he asked why I was using a butter knife instead of a screwdriver. I explained that I didn't have a screwdriver, but I had a drawer filled with butter knives. He left and returned five minutes later with several screwdrivers, including a cordless one. I was amazed at how easily and quickly I was able to finish the job. He explained that the right tools make all the difference. Who knew?

And it is the same with studying the Bible. It is one thing for scholars to study the Bible; but what's the average person supposed to do in order to understand the Bible? There are a number of excellent resources readily available to aid your study. A few include:

• The very first thing you need is a **Bible**! Don't laugh—you would be surprised how many people profess to study the Bible without actually having a Bible.

• In addition to the Bible, you may want to invest in a good **Bible dictionary**—there are a good many on the market. Three to consider include the one-volume *Eerdmans Dictionary of the Bible* (W.B. Eerdmans: Grand Rapids, MI 2000), which is richly illustrated and provides a wide range of theological perspectives; the highly respected one-volume *HarperCollins Bible Dictionary* (HarperSanFrancisco: San Francisco 1996), which includes comprehensive articles on the Dead Sea Scrolls and sixteen maps that highlight the politics and boundaries of biblical times; and *The New Interpreter's Dictionary of the Bible* (Abingdon Press: Nashville, TN c2006-), which features contributions by a diverse group of women and men representing a range of religious, geographical, theological, and cultural backgrounds.

• A **concordance** lists every word in the Bible alphabetically and directs you to all the passages where that word appears. Some also include each word's Hebrew or Greek roots. This tool provides a quick way of looking up a passage if you know only a word or phrase. Some are exhaustive and others will list just certain words. Be sure that your concordance is keyed to the version of the Bible you will use; otherwise, the words will not match. For instance, the most popular volume, *Strong's Exhaustive Concordance of the Bible* (Abingdon: Nashville, TN 1986), is keyed to the KJV; *The New International*

Bible Concordance (Zondervan Pub. House: Grand Rapids, MI 1998) is keyed to the NIV; and *The Concise Concordance to the New Revised Standard Version* (Oxford University Press: New York 1993) is keyed to the NRSV.

• A **commentary** will be helpful because it will provide a great deal of information for you—and that information is all in one place. Commentaries cover every book of the Bible and many will include the books of the Apocrypha as well. Some are designed for daily, weekly, or monthly study; others provide general overviews of the biblical books without trying to provide a devotional or personal study focus. Some commentaries include articles of interest and aids for teaching and preaching the biblical texts. There are some one-volume commentaries, but most are multi-volume sets. They can be expensive, so take some time to review them. You may want to mix your collection by picking and choosing from a number of series rather than investing in just one—do what is most helpful for you and your purposes. A few to consider: Fortress Press' *Hermeneia* series for a critical and serious look at scripture based on the interpretation of the original languages of the Bible and other closely related literature; the 52-volume *Word Biblical Commentary* (Thomas Nelson: Nashville, TN 1982-2005), which provides sound exegesis as well as applications to real life; a series from John Knox Press, *Interpretation: A Bible Commentary for Teaching and Preaching*, which also attempts to relate the biblical text to contemporary life; and a 12-volume set, *The New Interpreter's Bible* (Abingdon Press: Nashville, TN 1994-2004), which boasts a diverse group of scholars who provide their reflections on what the text can mean for us today from their various social, racial, gender, and theological contexts.

• An **atlas** or book of maps provides visuals of places mentioned in the Bible and a way of understanding how places relate to each other. Some might also include information about climate and land use. An atlas is especially helpful since many place names have changed over the years. Take a look at these: the *Zondervan NIV Atlas of the Bible* (Regency Reference Library: Grand Rapids, MI 1989), which contains more than 200 color photographs, illustrations, charts and maps along with a glossary and scripture index; *The HarperCollins Concise Atlas of the Bible* (HarperOne: New York 1997), which includes a chronology of events and indexes of names, places, and biblical references and contains over 250 maps, site reconstructions, and color photographs; and the latest *Oxford Bible Atlas* (Oxford University Press: New York 2007), which includes recent advances in biblical, archaeological, and topographical scholarship.

Reflection Questions

1. Do you have any favorite Bible verses? If so, tell why these passages hold meaning for you.

2. How do you plan to study the Bible? Be specific.

3. What Bible stories are highlighted in your denomination's statement of faith or your congregation's mission statement? How are these stories, images, or concepts lived out in your church's mission and worship?

Three

The Story of the Bible: A Quick Look

From Creation to Consummation

For many, the Bible is an intimidating book. Actually, the Bible is a collection of books that include different styles and genres, written by different authors over a long period of time, and shaped by different theological understandings that also reflect the social and political concerns of the times in which the materials were written. It would be easier to throw up our hands and say, "Forget about it!" But there is something compelling about the Bible—we can't ignore it that easily.

The biblical message itself is simple—something happened! And that "something" changed the religious landscape for all time. The people who experienced this "something" did not set out to create a new religion—they merely wanted to describe their understanding of what happened. They did what we all do—try to put words on an experience for which there are no words.

The central event, the something that happened, was their deliverance from slavery in Africa; yes, Egypt is in Africa! These people were a small group of nomads who had migrated to Egypt. Their situation went from good to bad and from bad to worse. They didn't have the power to free themselves and no one to rescue them from their servitude—they did what helpless people do. They cried out to whatever god would listen. Miraculously, there was a god listening. And that god had the power to change their situation—this group of Semitic people were freed from slavery and released into a new freedom. This "exodus" event galvanized the people to deepen the relationship with the god who rescued them. This god wanted more than a verbal thank-you or a Hallmark card. This god had demands and one of them was a close and personal relationship with the people. No relationship is perfect and this one has its ups and downs. Yet the relationship has endured all the challenges and continues to this day.

Most of us are familiar with some version of an age-old story of the six blind persons and the elephant, a story reportedly based on an ancient East Indian legend. Each individual explained what the elephant was like based on personal experience: one fell against the elephant's side and declared it was like a wall; the second felt the tusk and declared it was like a spear; the third felt the elephant's trunk and declared it was like a snake; the fourth felt the elephant's knee and declared it was like a tree; the fifth touched the elephant's ear and declared it was like a fan; the sixth felt the elephant's tail and declared it was like a rope. All were partly right and all were partly wrong—each knew only of individual experience and had no sense of the whole. And this happens sometimes when we study the Bible—sometimes it reads like a short story; other times, we encounter poetry that doesn't rhyme; some parts are like legal documents; other parts need a good editor to avoid the repetitions and convoluted sentences. The Bible is all this and more—and that's the challenge. How do we make sense of the whole when we know snippets and fragments of the story? This section is designed to give you the whole sweep of the biblical story.

It may be helpful to think of the Bible as a novel or a drama. The story line or plot of the Bible revolves around a series of turning points and decisive moments. The plot moves along a continuum that is traceable. The Bible story moves from the general to the specific. Israel experienced a liberatory event. This event dramatically changed the way they saw the world. Every subsequent experience was seen through the filter of their liberation. Their lives were indelibly changed and everything in the past, in the present, and in the future must be understood in light of this extraordinary experience.

So let's explore the series of moves—in sixty-six books (thirty-nine in the Hebrew Bible and twenty-seven in the New Testament), we see the following moments:

• **Creation**. In the beginning, there was God who made the heavens, the earth, and all that is. This part of the story sets the stage for the rest of the drama—God creates humankind and the experiment has its ups and downs. One of the downs included the expulsion of the humans from a beautiful garden. On their own, the humans make decisions—some wise, some not so wise. In this period of the story, we meet Adam and Eve, their sons Cain and Abel. We also meet Noah, Abraham, Sarah, and Hagar. We hear the promises God makes to Noah and to Abraham. And we wonder how God will pull these off: Noah was told to build a big boat and load up humans and animals—all on a clear summer day. Abraham was promised to be the father of many people—he was quite elderly and so was his wife who was also barren. We see the triangle formed when Sarah uses Hagar as a surrogate mother—then commands Abraham to send the slave girl and her child away. We see Abraham raise a knife to kill his second son, Isaac, as God commanded—then, at the last minute, Isaac is reprieved. We watch how Isaac and Rebekah handle their family situation and the rivalry between their two sons Esau and Jacob. We watch Jacob leave home under horrifying circumstances and how he labors for fourteen years for the woman of his dreams, only to find out that she is barren. We see how God makes a way for Rachel to give birth after her sister produces a number of children for Jacob. We watch Jacob's sons sell their brother, Joseph, into slavery—it seems that God's promises just might not come to pass. Then in the midst of a famine, Jacob moves his family to Egypt where Joseph has triumphed over every adversity. All the while, we see men and women who move both towards and away from God. And we see God who loves and is disappointed, who is remorseful yet hopeful about the capacity of humanity to do the right things for the right reasons. God assures Abraham, Isaac, and Jacob that their family will survive and will thrive in a land of their own—trust in God and God's promises was the key.

• **Captivity.** Jacob thrives despite the disappointments and delays. His sons form the Twelve Tribes of Israel. When the sons die, their children do well for a while—until Joseph dies. There arose a ruler over Egypt who had no memory of Joseph or his family. The Israelites became slaves and were treated harshly. God heard the cry of a captive people in Egypt. The Hebrews multiply and Pharaoh begins to worry about the possible rebellion of his free labor force. He plots to control the population but is undermined by two savvy midwives, Puah and Shiphrah. And there is the miraculous saving of Moses—who is adopted by Pharaoh's own daughter. Moses grows up in the royal palace but never forgets who he is. In exile, on the run for murder,

Moses has an encounter with God—between the burning bush and the voice from heaven, it's a wonder Moses didn't faint dead away. God commissions Moses to deliver the Hebrews from slavery in Africa and form a community to be governed by God. After much hemming and hawing, Moses consents and works with Aaron and Miriam to set God's people free.

• **Covenant.** God not only set the Israelites free, God insisted on having a personal relationship with them, a formal relationship with obligations and privileges. God established a covenant with the Israelites—God was a partner with humanity and God promised them a place they could call home. Israel's God was a jealous God and required total faithfulness, no messing around with other gods. The people gave lip service to fidelity, but they didn't quite get it right.

• **Conquest.** With the help of God, the Israelites settled into the land that God had promised them and they had quite an adventure reaching their homeland. Others occupied Canaan, the Promised Land, and Israel had the massive task of staking their claim in the land. But they were driven and supported by God who aimed to see them settled in the land. Here we find the stories of Joshua, Moses' replacement. At God's prompting, Joshua and Caleb constantly reminded the people that God was in charge of their lives and that God uses some unlikely persons to further God's cause. The story of Rahab is a case in point—she was a harlot (a prostitute) and was instrumental in Joshua's military strategy to occupy the land. This section of the Bible also deals with the judges—a series of charismatic leaders chosen and empowered by God to deal with immediate crises. Here we find the stories of Gideon, Deborah (a female judge!), Jephthah, and Samson among others.

• **Coronations.** Once they had settled in the land promised by God, the Israelites wanted to live like the nations that surrounded them; they wanted a king, a ruler, a monarch to take care of them. Their conquest of the land was difficult and continual skirmishes and threats from other nations created problems. Israel was a loose federation of tribes characterized by discord, jealousy and rancor. No longer satisfied with God's ways of raising charismatic leaders as the need arose, the people wanted the assurance of knowing someone was watching out for them all the time. The desire for a monarch in Israel was rooted in Hannah's prayer for a son. God "opened" her womb and she conceived and dedicated her son, Samuel, to God. Samuel was the last of the judges and an able prophet who regularly conversed with God. It was Samuel who conveyed the people's desire for a monarch. God granted their wish but had misgivings right from the beginning. Israel's first monarch was

Saul. His reign started well—he was a warrior and fought the good fight. But he didn't quite understand what it meant to be a ruler and he overstepped his bounds. He was replaced, rather unceremoniously, by God's chosen, David— according to scripture, David was handsome and good-looking, a brilliant warrior and visionary, and David loved God deeply. David pulled off establishing a political and religious center in Jerusalem. But David proved to be only too human—here we have stories of David's dalliance with Bathsheba, the subsequent murder of her husband Uriah, the prophet Nathan's call for accountability, and the death of the child conceived in David's violation of Bathsheba. David's family life took a downward spiral; he lived to a ripe old age, but there was great tension in his family. David was forbidden to build a temple to God. David's son, Solomon, was a wise ruler with great administrative skills—he built a magnificent temple for God and all seemed right with the world. Solomon's "flaw" was that he loved women from other nations and faith traditions—not a wise thing for Israel. The office of the prophet arose in an attempt to keep the rulers in check and to keep the people connected to their God—and they certainly had their hands full.

• **Calamity.** God's statement that there would always be a descendant of David on the throne in Israel was not enough to ensure the nation would last forever. Solomon, despite his administrative acumen, failed to set a standard of succession and after he died his sons fought over who should be the next king. The result was a divided nation—a Northern Kingdom (Israel) and a Southern Kingdom (Judah). And we all know that a house divided against itself cannot stand. Despite the warnings of the prophets, the people continued to disobey God and ignore the tenets of the covenant; it was inevitable, then, that both nations fell to greater imperial powers—the North to Assyria and the South to Babylon. The unthinkable had happened—the Israelites were displaced and sent into the Diaspora, a fate considered worse than death. God had forsaken the very people God had called into being.

• **Challenge.** The Israelites needed to understand what had happened to them. They wanted to know why their fate was so cruel. Where was God when the people needed God the most? Who was to blame for their circumstances? These are questions the prophets and psalmists sought to answer. Their answers would set the chart for the future of the broken nation. In this part of the story, we meet some colorful figures—Elijah, Ezekiel, Isaiah, Jeremiah, Amos, Joel, Habakkuk, Hosea—who pulled out all the stops to get the people's attention and to get them back on track in their relationship with God. It was an uphill climb and they experienced great frustration and exasperation. Despite their eccentric and often bizarre tactics to get the people's attention, the prophets were not able to get the monarchs on the right track. With just a few exceptions, the monarchs imposed heavy taxes on the people, exploited the people for their labor; class divisions developed with those of higher status and wealth reaping the benefits and privileges. In other words, Israel's divided life was a total mess!

• **Comfort.** Even in the midst of challenge, change and catastrophe, however, God continued to lurk in the background—listening, caring, and working to restore relationship with God's people. The people were left to live the consequences of their choices and decisions. God was faithful even when silent and seemingly absent. Here we see the theological wrestlings of Job and the Psalmist(s) as they try to help the people understand and survive their circumstances. The people displaced and in exile struggled to hold on to their faith, memory, and culture. There were no temple or pilgrimage gatherings in Jerusalem. Those in the Diaspora were left without the support and resources of the temple and its priests—they struggled to hold on to their religion and faith while they waited for freedom and restoration to their homeland. We see the work of restoration that so engaged Ezra and Nehemiah. We meet Esther and Ruth and we hear the wisdom of the Proverbs. Things are slowly coming back together. God had used Israel's enemies to teach the nation a lesson—despite a succession of superpowers, some friendlier to Israel's exiles than others, the people were not free. God was doing something; yet all was still not right. What was God up to in the world?

• **Christ.** Just when things were bleakest, God did something remarkable—God entered into the human experience. Through the work of John the Baptist, God prepared the way for a special messenger—not just any messenger, but the very Word of God, the Messiah, God's Anointed One, Jesus of Nazareth. God did not enter the human experience as a knight in shining armor or a great warrior with a fleet of chariots. These images were the fantasies of a people suffering under Roman domination. Instead of a great warrior monarch, God showed up as a babe laid in a manger, born in Bethlehem and raised in Nazareth. God entered the human experience heralded by shepherds and angels and magi from the East. Jesus did not set out to start a new religion—he aimed to reform Judaism and make the people live up to the covenant promises their ancestors had made to God—to feed the hungry, clothe the naked, give sight to the blind, activity of limbs to the lame, to set the captives free. Despite his own example as a role model, despite his teachings through parables, despite his miracle workings, the people didn't get him or his work. The people did not rise to the occasion. Instead, the religious powers of the day—Pharisees, Sadducees, scribes, and elders—threatened by his popularity, handed Jesus over to be crucified by the Roman authorities. It was a sad day, that Good Friday when Jesus was laid in a tomb. And if Jesus had stayed dead, he would have been a mere footnote in Israel's story. But Jesus was raised by God—resurrected—and a new movement began. This movement was inclusive of Jews and non-Jews (Gentiles). Solidly connected with and rooted in Jewish traditions, these followers of Jesus called themselves the "new" Israel and formed what eventually became the Christian church.

• **Church.** This new religion was based on egalitarian values and continued the standards set by Moses and the Ten Commandments but with a fresh perspective on what constituted the "household of God." The notion of a promised land gave way to the household (reign) of God—where all are welcomed. The "old" Israel has given way to a "new" Israel—with God's love written on their hearts, and liberated from the impossible demands of Mosaic law yet firmly rooted in it, too. God's people were given a choice to live in community—open, inclusive, loving—guided and sustained by God, Christ, and the Holy Spirit, sharing their goods and their gifts, exercising the fruit of the Spirit. The early church met in house churches, broke bread together, and praised God through hymns, the hearing of the scripture, and through preaching. The preachers and teachers of the Gospel spread the word that God had done something new in Jesus and that God continues to do a new thing throughout the cosmos. Here we find the letters of Paul and other teachers—helping the early Christians claim and clarify their identity and mission.

• **Consummation.** The Good News continues to be that God is not done with us yet! God continues to create and liberate and call us into community. God's reign has begun and will continue until Jesus returns. The book of the Revelation, a prophetic summons to get it together in preparation for Christ's return, begins with letters to seven churches. Revelation is filled with dramatic and fiery images and strange visions. The early church expected the Parousia (the Second Coming of Christ) to happen sooner rather than later. Early sermons and correspondences are marked with a sense of urgency; even Jesus, during his earthly ministry, preached that the Reign of God was upon us—now! But as the days turned into months and months into years and years into decades and decades into centuries—we have lost that sense of urgency. Now we must figure out how to live together until Jesus reappears. We haven't always done a good job—Protestant denominations continue to splinter and new religious groups form every day. As one preacher put it, if Christ is coming back for his church without a spot or a wrinkle, we have a lot of washing and ironing to do! Indeed, there is much work to be done if we are to be one united Church—we work as we wait for God's great consummation of God's purposes and intentions for creation.

This, in a nutshell, is the biblical story. It is a suspenseful one—filled with intrigue, disappointments, humor, struggle, gore, sex, murder, bad choices as well as mercy, grace, forgiveness, redemption, joy, and hope. The biblical story engages our minds, hearts, and souls—and should be preached and taught in ways that fully engage us. As we study the Bible, we wonder along the way, what God will do as the circumstances and conditions of God's people change. We wonder if the people will make decisions for God, if they will live up to God's expectations of them. Ultimately, these are the very questions that fuel our faith today—what is God up to in the world today and how will God cast us in the divine drama?

Reflection Questions

1. Why is it important for *you* to know more about the Bible?
2. What translation of the Bible do you prefer? Why?
3. How is the Bible used in public and political discourse?
4. For the next week, keep a list of biblical references you see and hear in the media. What does your list say about the Bible's influence on secular and religious life?

Four

The Story of the Bible: A Deeper Look

The Bible is a story—with a beginning and an ending, even though the ending is still being played out. This story moves along a continuum—there are ups and downs, colorful and flawed characters, mysterious and miraculous events and incidents, unpredictable and unpredicted outcomes. There are times when the story threatens to end prematurely. Then something else happens and we're off and running again. Our quick overview of the biblical story left out a lot of details, some of which we will fill in as we move through this chapter.

Most of us know something about the Bible. For instance, most us know, or think we know, the story of Adam and Eve, Cain and Abel—the first family of the Bible. Most of us know the story of Abraham, Sarah, and Isaac. Most of us have heard of Jacob and Esau and the infamous bowl of stew. We know that Noah built a big boat to save humanity and the animal world from the great flood. We know of Jonah who was swallowed by a big fish—we know snippets of stories but very often our details are fuzzy. For example, there is no mention of an apple or sin in the biblical story of Adam and Eve. The Bible says a fish, not a whale, swallowed Jonah. And there are many other examples of popular "knowledge" versus what the Bible actually says.

In the following chapters, we will take a closer look at some Bible stories that all Christians should be familiar with—these are stories we can't live without.

The formative event for the Jewish legacy of our Judeo-Christian tradition is the exodus, the deliverance from slavery to freedom. The Israelites knew a God who liberated them. This God heard their cry because of their oppression and acted in the concreteness of history to respond to their cry. Knowing what they knew in light of that event, what could they say about God who hears, responds, and liberates? They knew God as a liberator, but what else might God be? Every moment and event was now understood against the backdrop of a personal God who was involved in their everyday lives. Not only that, now these moments and events also carried theological meaning. For the next few pages, we will explore some highlights of the biblical story, paying attention to major characters, themes, and outcomes.

The Bible is one of the most fascinating books ever written. The Bible does not, however, give detailed instructions on what we are supposed to do or how we are supposed to live. It is composed of public documents written primarily by men, primarily for men, about the nature of God's relationship with and to humanity. The Bible tells us about a God who loves us and saves us by God's grace despite who we are and what we do. The Bible is a witness that contains stories of triumph, trials, troubles, failures, and victories. It is a witness to a God who is and who creates; a Christ who cares and redeems; and a Holy Spirit that comforts and guides.

Bible study helps us gain glimpses into who God is and how God deals with us. Further, Bible study helps us to see ourselves more clearly in light of God's gracious and merciful dealings with us. Remember that we don't come to the Bible as blank slates—we bring our own experiences, biases, judgments, prejudices, insecurities, and wisdom to each study.

Far from being boring, the Bible is filled with interesting characters, life-changing scenarios, sticky situations, and unpredictable outcomes. How can we not connect with the son or daughter who feels that mom loved the other sibling best? How can we justify a father's decision to slit his only son's throat? How can we ignore the pleas of a man who is commanded to marry a prostitute in a culture where virgin brides are the expected, the only acceptable choice? How can we ignore a married woman who is caught in the very act of having sex with a man who is not her husband yet her partner in crime is exonerated? How can we fail to empathize with a man who is unjustly hung for an imaginary crime? Are these all plots for a new reality show or mini-series on television? Not even close—these are all stories in the Bible! Don't you want to know what happens to Jacob and Esau? Abraham and Isaac? Hosea and Gomer? The woman caught in adultery? Jesus of Nazareth? A good Bible study class will help you find out what happens to these people.

Their stories are interesting, to say the least; they are instructive, too. There are clues and lessons for living that we can glean from our biblical ancestors, for their story is our story. God is continually doing a new thing and God invites us to join the journey. Let's take a closer look at some of these specific moments and see what we can learn.

Unfortunately, it is beyond the scope of this volume to provide a comprehensive set of Bible studies. Instead, in the following chapters, we have selected some passages to stand as representatives of the major divisions of the Bible. The passages have been chosen for one or more of the following reasons:

• They illustrate some aspect of the overall biblical story—personality, plot, theology, etc.

• They lend themselves to a fresh interpretation from the more popular or traditional understandings of the text.

• They illustrate or challenge how we are to live as people of God in the twenty-first century CE.

Each study follows a pattern: selection to be read; short overview of the text's larger context; brief comments about the text itself; a short commentary on why we need this passage; and reflection questions for discussion and meditation. Individuals or groups may use these studies. Have a great time exploring these texts!

Five

Torah/Pentateuch

Then God said, "Let us make humankind in our image,
according to our likeness; and let them have dominion over the fish
of the sea, and over the birds of the air, and over the cattle, and
over all the wild animals of the earth, and over every creeping thing
that creeps upon the earth." (Genesis 1:26.)

In the beginning...Read Genesis 3:1-24

Genesis is the book of beginnings: of the universe, of the community Israel, and of faith. It includes the period from creation to Israel's sojourn in Egypt. It is divided into two major sections:

* Genesis 1–11 is primeval history; its scope is universal; it tells how God enabled humans to multiply and populate the earth;
* Genesis 12–50 is ancestral history; it tells of Israel's ancestors— Abraham, Sarah, Hagar (Genesis 12-25); Isaac, Rebekah, Esau and Jacob (Genesis 26-36); and Joseph (Genesis 37-50).

In the book of Genesis, we have a declaration about how the world came into being. But we are immediately confronted with the complexity of the Bible— we have two different creation stories, each from a different perspective and tradition. Scholars generally agree that Genesis 1–3 was shaped during the exile rather than by a period soon after the creation event itself.

45

The first creation story, Genesis 1:1–2:3, is generally believed to be the work of the Priestly tradition, usually denoted "P." God speaks the world into being and creates humans in the divine image and likeness. God gives the humans two primary tasks: to be fruitful and multiply and to have stewardship over the rest of creation. The P tradition gives us a picture of an orderly creative process and emphasizes the equality between man and woman.

The second creation story, Genesis 2:4–25, is shaped by the Yahwist tradition, known as "J." This conclusion is partly based on the shift in how God is designated. Here, God is *YHWH* Elohim, often translated as "LORD God" in English Bibles. In this creation story, the earth is lifeless except for water. God creates man from the dust and breathes life into him. God places him in a garden where there are two trees from which he is not to eat: the tree of life and the tree of the knowledge of good and evil. God creates living creatures to keep the man company but none of them proves to be a suitable companion. After man has named the creatures, God puts him to sleep and extracts a rib from which God creates woman. The man and woman live in innocent harmony; see Genesis 2:25.

This text is popularly referred to as the "fall" of humanity and is supposed to deal with "the original sin"—the humans did what was evil in God's sight and are condemned to eternal punishment. You will note that sin is not mentioned in the text; that there is no mention of a "fall" from God's grace; and that the humans eat a piece of fruit, not an apple! The doctrine of Original Sin associated with this passage was popularized by an early church patriarch, Augustine of Hippo in Africa. He offered an interpretation of the text that has become part of the Christian tradition. The text itself, however, says nothing to this effect.

Additionally, some interpret this passage to mean that women are destined to be subordinate to men. Feminist and Womanist scholars, however, suggest another understanding. This *particular* woman is sentenced (no explicit curse is indicated in the text) to a subordinate role to a *particular* man because of their mutual disobedience, not because God instituted or ordained such hierarchy for society. The status of the woman and the man has shifted from equal partners because *they* sinned; the text does not say that the woman is more sinful than the man; the text does not say that the woman is responsible for the fall from grace of all humanity. She and the man are sentenced to the consequences of their actions.

They are banished from the garden and left to live a life of challenge—as do all humans. Contemporary scholars suggest that this story is about growing up—if the man and woman are to understand the full range of what it means to be human (and to be created in the image and likeness of God), they have to go through some things that force them to grow and stretch their understandings of the world. God has given humans both freedom and limits.

The biblical storyteller in Genesis makes no attempt to harmonize the two creation stories—they stand as a testimony to the diversity of perspectives we find throughout the Bible. Each story carries theological implications. The theological bottom line is that God is Creator—of the cosmos and of human life. Further, God grants freedom to humans—to choose and make decisions. And God allows humans to live the consequences of their choices. The key to life, then, is complete and total reliance on God, otherwise, life is filled with alienation, separation, disunity and disharmony. Instead of open, caring and loving relationships, we deal with suspicions, distrust, anger, shame and hostility. To choose God is the better way; but we have a difficult time remembering that. Even in choices that resist God's gifts, God still finds ways to provide—the naked man and woman are given clothes; the man and woman, banished from the garden, still have skills to make their way in the world, even in the face of a changed reality. Despite our choices, God provides.

Why We Need this Story

It is important to know this story because of the way it has been misused— it has shaped the ways in which societies view women and it's been bad for women. Male-dominated and male-focused cultures use this text to justify the subjugation and oppression of women. However, a closer look flies in the face of such interpretations. Instead of being docile and submissive, the woman in this text is vocal, thoughtful, creative, fearless, smart, takes the initiative, and makes a contribution. The text doesn't talk about sin or the fall of humanity, though it has been interpreted that way. It may be difficult to shift the paradigm—most of us have grown up with the notion of a sinful humanity deeply ingrained in our minds and hearts. Many do not feel worthy of God's love and don't fully grasp what grace is all about. A careful reading of the text shows that God provides freedom, choice, and limitations. As creatures who mirror the image and likeness of God, we are given the opportunity to decide—for God or against God—we always have a choice. The difficulty lies in our willingness to live with the choices we make; therein is the real freedom. Despite, or even because of, our choices, God remains present and faithful—and therein is the real meaning of grace!

Reflection Questions

1. What message do you think the biblical writer wants to convey in Genesis 3?

2. Does God's "punishment" of the man, the woman, and the serpent fit the "crime"? Explain your answer.

3. What portrait of God emerges from Genesis 3? What are God's "weaknesses" and "strengths" in this story?

4. How does this story influence or shape your perceptions of women?

5. What do you believe about "original sin"? How does this text support your belief?

▼ ▼ ▼

> Then [YHWH] said, "I have observed the misery of my people who are in Egypt; I have heard their cry on account of their taskmasters. Indeed, I know their sufferings, and I have come down to deliver them from the Egyptians, and to bring them up out of that land to a good and broad land, a land flowing with milk and honey..."
> (Exodus 3:7–8a.)

The Essence of Community Life...Read Exodus 20:1-17

The heart of the Torah and Hebrew Bible is the book of Exodus. It deals with Israel's freedom from Egypt and the subsequent wilderness wandering. All Jewish tradition goes back to this formative experience; it is the point at which Israel became a community. Israel began as a nomadic band of people on the move like many other peoples at that time. Because of the Exodus, however, Israel became a community in intimate relationship with a God who was actively involved in history on their behalf. Exodus, the book of the exit, is the story of Moses' call by God to rescue God's people from oppression in Egypt. Moses stands at the center of this book. He was called to be the prophetic interpreter of God's liberating action and to be the priestly mediator of the covenant between God and God's people.

Israel's captivity in Egypt continues the story of Jacob's family that began in Genesis. The immediate background is the family's departure from Canaan during a famine and their settlement in Egypt on land granted by the king (Genesis 46-47). Exodus tells how YHWH was faithful with the promises made to the ancestors and how God rescued their descendants from slavery.

The focus of this section of the Bible is on Moses—the liberator of his people. His choices were crucial to God's work on behalf of Israel. His sister miraculously saved Moses from extermination—she placed Moses in a basket and floated him on the Nile River where Pharaoh's daughter found him. Pharaoh was slaughtering other boys under two years old because of the subversive work of two Hebrew midwives, Shiphrah and Puah, who feared God. Moses grew up in the palace but never forgot his heritage. He murdered an Egyptian who was abusing a Hebrew—Moses came to the rescue of his fellow Hebrew. He realized that he was guilty and that Pharaoh was looking to kill him. Moses fled Egypt and settled in Midian where he worked for Jethro and married his daughter, Zipporah. Time passed and Moses experienced a theophany, a physical appearance of and communication with God—this is the famous "burning bush" event. The event is all the more remarkable because God reveals the divine name to Moses:

> But Moses said to God, "If I come to the Israelites and say to them, 'The God of your ancestors has sent me to you,' and they ask me, 'What is his name?' what shall I say to them?" God said to Moses, "I AM WHO I AM." He said further, "Thus you shall say to the Israelites, 'I AM has sent me to you.'" God also said to Moses, "Thus you shall say to the Israelites, [YHWH], the God of your ancestors, the God of Abraham, the God of Isaac, and the God of Jacob, has sent me to you': This is my name forever, and this my title for all generations." (Exodus 3:13–15.)

Moses was commanded by God to return to Egypt to free the Hebrew slaves. Moses didn't want the job, but God had an answer to every one of Moses' objections. God would not be put off; God provided what Moses needed to do the work that God had for him. After a series of dramatic encounters with Pharaoh, Moses led the people out of Egypt.

The Exodus, the formative event, is marked by three periods: (a) a period of temporary residence in the land of Canaan (ancestral sojourn); (b) a period of exclusion from the land (residence and captivity in Egypt); and, (c) a period of preparation for a return to the land (wilderness). These three periods are followed by a triumphal reentry into the land and its conquest and settlement under Joshua's leadership.

Our focus passage, Exodus 20:1–17, is popularly referred to as the "Ten Commandments." It is also known as the Decalogue or Ten Words. It is mostly the result of the J and Elohist ("E") traditions, and the events and words it portrays happened centuries before the written form was finalized. The Decalogue, based on Israel's covenant with God, most resembles the suzerainty treaties used in ancient times. A suzerainty treaty was used in the socio-political life of Israel's neighbors who were organized into city-states. These treaties enabled the people to live in relative harmony with each other. Most treaties were between a major power and a subordinate city.

The theme of Exodus centers on *covenant* (in Hebrew, *berit*, which means "cutting," "binding," "eating"). A covenant, like a suzerainty treaty, is an agreement or bond between two parties: (a) when the agreement is between equals, obligations and privileges are shared equally; (b) when the agreement is between unequal parties (such as ruler and subjects or a lord and servants), a promise is made by the stronger party and the weaker party must meet certain obligations and demands. There is no doubt about God's power and presence—God means to be in relationship with Israel. In this case, the treaty between God and Israel is not negotiated; God offers the terms of the agreement and Israel must uphold its end of the deal.

The Decalogue sets forth the essence of community life for Israel. It outlines Israel's expected response to God's deliverance from bondage—loyalty to God and harmonic life with each other. The exodus is to be understood as God's decisive action on behalf of Israel and it is the first word for Israel—see Exodus 20:2-3. Given God's act of liberation, God now encourages community. A wandering group of diverse people has been freed to form community—the Ten Commandments outline how that community should behave.

Within the guidelines for community, God makes it clear that for Israel, there is only one God—all others are to be rejected. While other people worship human and animal representations of their gods, Israel is to hold the memory of what God has done on their behalf and not some image of their making.

Also within the community guidelines is the need for balance—in one's personal and communal life. The Sabbath is to be a time of rest—a notion that is lost in the hustle and bustle of our lives today. We can barely slow down, let alone rest—there's so much to do. But if we are to live by the Ten Commandments (as some branches of Christianity declare), businesses would shut down one day a week and all work would cease. I remember a time when we had to get all of our shopping done on Saturdays because all the stores, gas stations, drugstores, department stores were closed on Sundays. In most communities now, Sunday is business as usual.

Note that the Bible does not deny the existence of other gods. Also, the words in the Decalogue are directed to the men (the "you" is in the masculine second-person—"you men"). Further, scholars suggest that while verse 13 prohibits killing (or murder), it does not include "legitimate" forms of killing, such as collateral damage in war, capital punishment methods, or defense against threats to Israel's safety, integrity, or holiness. (The Hebrew word for kill used here is *rasah*, instead of the more common *harag*, and it allows for a wider range of interpretations.) And, in verse 14 the word "steal" is not simply about theft or loss of property; it also implies kidnapping and thus applies to human and animal "property."

Why We Need this Story

This part of the Bible is among the most quoted. Even those with only a cursory understanding of the Bible know about the Ten Commandments. No doubt part of this knowledge is due to Cecil B. DeMille's Oscar-winning film by the same name. In addition, many of our civil laws are based on understandings of the Ten Commandments. Even in everyday conversation, we will often make reference to one of the commandments.

So important are these instructions that they are repeated in Deuteronomy 5:6–21. The instructions are elaborated upon in the books of Leviticus, Numbers and Deuteronomy. These commandments should govern our lives—as a joyous response to all that God has done and is doing on our behalf. We often fall short of the ideal community because of our egos, insecurities, greed and lack of love for one another. God holds the ideal before us and we still have a choice to make in how we will live together.

Reflection Questions

1. What message do you think the biblical writer is trying to convey in Exodus 20?

2. How do you react to these "commandments"? Explain your answer.

3. How closely do you follow these commandments?

4. What picture of God emerges from this passage?

5. What is God calling you to do? Are you happy about the call or are you resisting it? Explain your answer.

Six

The Former Prophets

*Before [Joshua's spies] went to sleep, [Rahab] came up to them on
the roof and said to the men: "I know that [YHWH] has given you the
land, and that dread of you has fallen on us, and that all the inhabitants
of the land melt in fear before you. For we have heard how [YHWH]
dried up the water of the Red Sea before you when you came out of
Egypt, and what you did to the two kings of the Amorites that were
beyond the Jordan, to Sihon and Og, whom you utterly destroyed. As
soon as we heard it, our hearts melted, and there was no courage left in
any of us because of you. [YHWH] your God is indeed God in heaven
above and on earth below." (Joshua 2:8–11.)*

Wherever I Hang My Hat is Home...Read Joshua 23:1–16

The book of Joshua outlines the history of Israel's conquest and settlement
of the land west of the Jordan under Joshua's leadership. Joshua 23 is his last
address to Israel and restates the Deuteronomic understanding of the time
period. Joshua's speech is designed to keep the people inspired and motivated
by recalling God's liberating action on their behalf.

In the book of Deuteronomy, Moses passed the mantle of leadership to
Joshua. The Israelites moved into Canaan, which was already occupied by
organized and civilized peoples. In Canaan, the form of government was the
city-state which was hierarchical with a privileged ruling class. In contrast,

Israel was organized into rural, tribal leagues, a kind of extended family (clan, tribe) with all having relatively equal status.

Religiously, Canaan was polytheistic (many gods) with "El" as chief god who was called "father bull" and creator. El was "married" to Asherah. Their chief son, "Baal" (meaning "lord") was the reigning ruler of gods believed to control heaven, earth and fertility. Israel believed in one God, YHWH. In Canaan, child sacrifice, religious prostitution and snake worship were common practices. Israel was warned to destroy these "wicked" people. (See Leviticus 18:24–28; 20:23; Deuteronomy 12:31; 20:17, 18.)

Israel's new leader, Joshua, was a ready and experienced leader (see Exodus 17:8–16, Numbers 13–14); in some ways, he was like Moses. He was assured success if he heeded the instructions given in the "book of the law" through Moses. There was a successful invasion of the land under Joshua's leadership. The book of Joshua describes a long, complicated process of conquest, or displacement of the Canaanites and other people who were occupying the land. The biblical story does not reflect what actually happened, historically speaking; some things are left out and others are re-arranged. The "author" uses an idealized historical narrative to describe Israel, past and future, in its relationship with God and the kind of society Israel wished to be.

The book of Joshua has three major divisions: chapters 1–12 describe the settlement of Israelite tribes in Canaan because of the successful military campaign led by Joshua; chapters 13–21 report the distribution of the land among the victorious tribes; chapters 22–24 is a collection of three stories that focus on loyalty that Israelite tribes owe to God who has given the land.

Joshua's farewell speech echoes that of Moses and rehearses God's action, reminds Israel of its covenant obligations, and warns of consequences of failing to keep its end of the deal. The major themes of the book include: (a) the conquest was the action of God; God worked through Rahab and despite the spies' doubts; (b) "Holy War," the total (utter) destruction of the enemy, was an act of worship (see Deuteronomy 20); (c) the community bore the guilt of an individual (see the Achan incident in Joshua 7); (d) the possession of the land is conditional upon faithfulness to God's "law"; (e) covenant curses may yet come to pass; (f) Israel's morality is a response to God's gift; and (g) the realization that Israel has entered into a close relationship with its God.

54

Why We Need this Story

The people of God have been through some stuff! They have endured tortuous times in Egypt, experienced a miraculous liberation, suffered through forty years of wilderness wanderings, and fought mightily to occupy the land they believed God had promised. And through it all, God provided—God made a way through the Sea of Reeds (the Red Sea) with Pharaoh's massive army nipping at their heels; God made a way by providing manna and water in the desert; God made a way by providing a pillar of fire and a pillar of clouds to serve as navigation systems; God made a way by using non-believers and a sex worker to provide safety for spies. Now that they are in the land, Israel still has work to do in order to settle in. Joshua reminds them that their task is not to occupy the land for wealth or status—their task is to be a model of community life governed by God. Israel's task is to show how good life can be when God is the head of state—by living out the Ten Commandments, Israel sets itself a part from the lawless, egocentric, greed-ridden nations that surrounded it.

It was a difficult task. We find the nation time and time again missing the mark that God has set—the people cannot embody the instructions of the Torah, they can't stay consistently connected to God. They constantly forget who they are and whose they are. It is no accident or mere coincidence that God utters these words so many times in the Bible, "Do not fear." The people have short memories and are often reminded that they are a people whom God has chosen and that God has not abandoned them. Both Moses and Joshua remind the people as they close out their respective careers: as in years past, the people are faced with a choice. Joshua makes the choice clear:

> *"Now therefore revere [YHWH], and serve him in sincerity and in faithfulness; put away the gods that your ancestors served beyond the River and in Egypt, and serve [YHWH]. Now if you are unwilling to serve [YHWH], choose this day whom you will serve, whether the gods your ancestors served in the region beyond the River or the gods of the Amorites in whose land you are living; but as for me and my household, we will serve [YHWH]."*
> (Joshua 24:14–15.)

Reflection Questions

1. What kind of leader was Joshua?
2. How do you rate Joshua's last political speech? What are its strengths? What are its weaknesses?

3. How do you think Native Americans, as displaced and annihilated peoples, would interpret this passage?

4. What picture of God emerges from this passage?

5. How does the story of the conquest impact current conflicts in the Middle East?

After [Elkanah and Hannah] had eaten and drunk at Shiloh, Hannah rose and presented herself before [YHWH]. Now Eli the priest was sitting on the seat beside the doorpost of the temple of [YHWH]. She was deeply distressed and prayed to [YHWH], and wept bitterly. She made this vow: "O [YHWH] of hosts, if only you will look on the misery of your servant, and remember me, and not forget your servant, but will give to your servant a male child, then I will set him before you as a nazirite until the day of his death. He shall drink neither wine nor intoxicants, and no razor shall touch his head." (1 Samuel 1:9–11.)

Like the Other Nations...Read 2 Samuel 5:1–12

After Joshua died, Israel entered a period of the "judges." The book of Judges is the history of Israelite tribal life under leaders called judges (in Hebrew, *sopetim*). The book represents a transition period. The age of the great leaders, Moses and Joshua, was over. The age of greatness under David is yet to come. The leaders of this period, the judges, were courageous but had their flaws and did not always follow the ways of God. The judges—including Gideon, Deborah, and Samson—were chosen and empowered by YHWH to be leaders.

Judges exercised leadership in the various tribes that made up Israel. Tribal identification was rooted in the legacy of Jacob—he is the father of twelve sons and one daughter. The sons represent the twelve tribes of Israel (while his daughter is not included) and these tribes would grow into a mighty nation and occupy land that God promised to Abraham. Here are Jacob's children:

The Children of Jacob

Name	Meaning of Name	Mother
Reuben	"behold, a son"	Leah
Simeon	"to hear"	Leah
Levi	"joined"	Leah
Judah	"praised"	Leah
Dan	"judge"	Bilhah
Naphtali	"my wrestling"	Bilhah
Gad	"good fortune"	Zilpah
Asher	"happy"	Zilpah
Issachar	"one for hire"	Leah
Zebulun	"exalt "	Leah
Dinah	"justice"	Leah
Joseph	"may Jehovah add"	Rachel
Benjamin	"son of the right hand"	Rachel

Joseph's territory was divided between two of his sons, Manasseh and Ephraim. We learn from the book of Judges that the conquest was not simple or complete; there were on-going battles and disputes with the people in Canaan. God raised up charismatic leaders whose function was to deliver God's people from their so-called "pagan" oppressors because of the difficulty of occupying the land. Joshua had warned the people that they owed their total allegiance to YHWH who delivered them from bondage; their failure to remain faithful to God would result in defeat and hard times. The book of Judges bears witness to this in its rendering of a four-fold repeated pattern in Israel: sin, sorrow, supplication and salvation. In other words, Israel would fall short of its covenant obligations, would be oppressed by an enemy, would cry out because of its oppression. God would raise a judge who would defeat the oppressor, there would be a period of well being and peace; then the people would fall short again and the pattern would repeat.

The book of Judges ends with the words, "In those days, there was no king (in Hebrew, *melek*) in Israel; all the people did what was right in their own eyes." (Judges 21:25.) Without strong central leadership dedicated to sustaining an "Israel" united in obedience to YHWH, the people lapsed into idolatrous practices. The tribal league that once triumphed over superior external enemies was torn apart by increasing bitter, bloody inter-tribal strife and conflict (see Judges 19–21).

There is some ambivalence about the monarchy in the scriptures. There are passages, on the one hand, that portray the royal office and its early monarchs in a favorable light: Saul and especially David are celebrated as YHWH's elect who, endowed with unusual measures of divine spirit, lead Israel to new heights of victory over its enemies. Royal leadership brings security, territorial gains and increasing wealth to the nation (see 1 Samuel 10:1, 23-26; 13:2–4; 14:47–48; 16:12–13; 2 Samuel 8:1–14). On the other hand, the monarchy is viewed negatively, as being itself an idolatrous institution, a sinful accommodation to the political practices and religious values of other nations. At best, some texts affirm human rulers although their very presence compromised YHWH's divine rule over Israel; at worst, monarchs may lead the covenant people into apostasy, threatening their very existence. While the exercise of royal authority may promote national unity and security, it inevitably poses the concrete threat of human tyranny.

The rapid transition from tribal league to monarchical state and empire had a profound effect upon Israel's theology and worship. The transition also affected its political, social and economic lives. In Israel, the monarch was to be a "servant" of YHWH. The Deuteronomistic perspective joins David and Zion (the name for Jerusalem, David's capital city in Judah) into the broad framework of the Mosaic covenant.

God reluctantly agreed to provide a monarch for Israel. Saul's reign was monitored by God and by the prophet Samuel. David came to the throne amid great turmoil, but he represents the highest expression of a monarch under the rule of YHWH. The covenant first made with Abraham, Isaac and Jacob, then refined and developed through Moses, continued to shape a nation that was to be a light to all other nations.

Some major themes include: the monarchy is rooted in the prayer of a barren woman, Hannah (see 1 Samuel 1:1–27); Samuel was the last judge and a fitting representative of God (see 1 Samuel 7:7–17); wanting a monarch was a big mistake (see 1 Samuel 8:10–22, 12:19); David, though flawed, was a man who deserved God's favor (see 1 Samuel 13:14, 16:13, 24:16–21).

Early on, the establishment of the monarchy appeared to be a divinely ordained blessing that was needed in order for Israel to maintain control and possession of the land. The monarchy was a precarious venture that threatened to undermine and undo the primary covenant bond between YHWH and Israel but also which had potential to bring the ancient promises of divine sovereignty and blessing to fulfillment.

At first, David was ruler over Judah only (2 Samuel 1–4) and later became ruler over Judah and Israel (2 Samuel 5–24). He was the most outstanding monarch in Israel's history for he was both political and religious—in a brilliant move, he established a capital city, Jerusalem, in neutral territory that did not belong to any of the Twelve Tribes. In this way, no tribe could claim special favors. In addition to establishing an administrative capital city, David relocated Israel's primary religious symbol, the Ark of the Covenant, to Jerusalem. The city, Zion, was now the religious center of the nation.

David proved to be an outstanding leader—he united the tribes of Israel into one effective union. He also organized the priests and Levites for effective participation in the ritual and ceremonial activities of the nation. The second book of Samuel tells of his reign in great detail, including dramatic tales of sin, crime, and rebellion in the royal family.

It is important to note that God made a covenant with David. For his loyalty and fidelity to God and God's ways, God granted David an eternal dynasty. There would always be a descendant of David on the throne. This covenantal understanding will be extremely important when the nation splits into two kingdoms.

Although he was an effective military man and political administrator, David was not able to manage his personal life well—read about the Uriah, Bathsheba, and Nathan incident in 2 Samuel 11:2–12:12. His personal life was filled with family tragedy and strife.

Why We Need this Story

This passage is important because it sets the stage for the action that follows. What we see is a nation that just can't seem to get and keep itself together. Despite all that God has done, Israel longs to be like other nations—Israel wants the stability and security human leaders are supposed to provide. They look at other nations and they see centralized governments, standing armies, military might, broad public works, and they wish to keep up with the Joneses. They are reluctant to maintain their uniqueness on the world stage. They are willing to give up some of their freedom for the security according to the world of their day. Israel continues to show that it cannot be trusted to remember and live out God's purpose for them. Please note that God honors Israel's choice for a ruler—and Israel will pay dearly for this choice.

Reflection Questions

1. What needs do the people seek to fulfill by crowning David monarch over Israel and Judah?

2. Describe David's leadership as shown in this passage. What are his strengths and what are his weaknesses?

3. How does the biblical writer portray David in this passage? Is he viewed positively or negatively? How can you tell?

4. What picture of God emerges in this passage?

5. In what ways does David's infamous encounter with Bathsheba and Nathan mirror contemporary political life?

Seven

The Latter Prophets

Have you not known? Have you not heard?
[YHWH] is the everlasting God,
the Creator of the ends of the earth.
[The Holy One] does not faint or grow weary;
[God's] understanding is unsearchable.
[God] gives power to the faint,
and strengthens the powerless.
Even youths will faint and be weary,
and the young will fall exhausted;
but those who wait for [YHWH] shall renew their strength,
they shall mount up with wings like eagles,
they shall run and not be weary,
they shall walk and not faint. (Isaiah 40:28-31.)

Following **the golden age of David's reign, Solomon becomes ruler.** There are high hopes for his reign; but trouble looms for Solomon, the monarchy, and Israel. The books of 1 and 2 Kings, originally one book, continue the story of the monarchy started in 1 and 2 Samuel and give an account of the Israelite kingdoms from the death of David, Solomon's tenure as ruler, the subsequent division of the nation, and the Exile. First and Second Kings deal with political history but emphasize the religious failure that led to the loss of national identity and freedom. The fall of both Israel and Judah is interpreted as the judgment of YHWH.

One of Solomon's accomplishments was the building of the Temple as a permanent place of worship. The Temple was built on top of Mt. Moriah directly north of Zion where David built his palace. It stood until Nebuchadnezzar destroyed it in 586 BCE; it was rebuilt in 520–515 BCE and demolished by Rome in 70 CE. A Muslim mosque, the Dome of the Rock, now sits there. The Temple was a magnificent structure and the dedication of the Temple was the most significant event in the religious history of Israel since the people left Mt. Sinai (see 1 Kings 8:6, 10–21).

Upon Solomon's death, the nation Israel split into two nations:

• Israel was the northern kingdom with ten tribes (see 1 Kings 12 to 2 Kings 17); its capital city was Samaria.

• Judah was the southern kingdom with two tribes, Judah and Benjamin; its capital city was Jerusalem.

The section of the Hebrew Bible known as the Latter Prophets deals with the classical prophets of Israel. They are a diverse group of men and women who regularly preached and taught from their own lives and experiences what God would have God's people do. Over a long period of time, these extraordinary persons refused to be satisfied with the status quo and dared to voice their feelings about life under God's rule. The monarchy threatened to displace God as the sovereign over Israel. The prophets' job was to make sure the people lived up to their covenantal responsibilities. When they failed to do so, the prophet called them to repent and renew their pledge of allegiance to God.

The task of the prophet was to mediate and interpret the divine mind and will. Prophetic communications were most often manifested in dreams, visions and ecstatic or mystical experiences. Biblical tradition traced prophecy back to Moses. In the Pentateuch (first five books of the Bible), the title of *nabi*, prophet, is given to Moses, Aaron, Miriam, and Deborah. The early function of the prophet was to stimulate patriotic and religious fervor.

The basic literary prophetic unit is a proclamation of judgment or salvation. Placed in the divine first-person and introduced with the formulaic expression, "Thus says YHWH" or "The word of YHWH came to me," prophecy is considered the very word of God. Usually, prophecy highlights some aspect of the Torah ("law") and its communal requirements. The prophets, then, serve as prosecutors in God's "lawsuit" or "controversy" against the people whom God had chosen. The people breached their end of the covenant and God called them to account for their actions. The prophets worked for God to spur the people to repentance. The Torah was used to "prove" that the people had violated God's "law" by forsaking God and by failing to live according to the teachings of the Torah.

The Latter Prophets are not placed in chronological order in the Bible. A rough chronological order of the prophets who pre-date the Babylonian exile would be: Amos, Hosea, "First" Isaiah, Micah, Nahum, Zephaniah, Habakkuk, Jeremiah, and Ezekiel. ("First Isaiah" refers to one of three prophets whose work is believed to be collected in the book that we call "Isaiah.") All except Hosea are from Judah (the Southern Kingdom where David's eternal dynasty is lodged), although Amos is a prophet who continues the Northern tradition of prophecy begun by Samuel and Elijah. There are many unnamed prophets, see Jeremiah 7:25, 11:7.

The post-exile prophets in rough chronological order are: "Second" and "Third" Isaiah, Haggai, Zechariah (Chapters 1–8), Malachi, Obadiah, Joel, and Zechariah (Chapters 9–11, 12–14).

In the Hebrew Bible, the prophetic books are seen as supplements to history. The prophets chastised the monarchs and tried to shape national policy by reminding the people that God longed for justice and peace (*shalom*). Further, the tasks of prophecy were: (a) to explain the massive disasters that befell the covenant people of God; (b) to serve as reminders of God's judgment and justice; and, (c) to lead the people back to the moral requirements of their covenant relationship.

The prophets reminded the people that underneath God's anger, disappointment, and judgment are also God's assurance of salvation, redemption and freedom. God is willing to give the people another chance, if they are truly repentant and willing to try again to live up to their covenantal responsibilities. True prophecy sometimes went unfulfilled and this was discouraging even to the prophets (see Jeremiah 20:7 ff). It was the word itself that must find a response in the heart open to God's invitation of grace. Much of prophecy had a messianic view. Israel had a history of looking for and expecting a savior and deliverer that started in the time of Moses and the judges. The expectation for a Messiah continues for modern Jews. However, after the prophet Daniel, the high inspiration of prophets was exhausted and Israel had to wait for a new outpouring of God's spirit. They wait for 400 years before YHWH breaks the silence!

▼ ▼ ▼

If I say, "I will not mention him,
or speak any more in his name,"
then within me there is something like a burning fire
shut up in my bones;
I am weary with holding it in,
and I cannot..." (Jeremiah 20:9.)

What's the Worst that Can Happen...Read Isaiah 43:15–21

The book of Isaiah consists of 66 chapters and is a composite work of several different voices, prophets who lived in different historical periods. The book is divided into three major parts:

• Chapters 1–39 are called "First Isaiah" and are attributed to the eighth century BCE prophet from Judah for whom the book is named.

• Chapters 40–55 are called "Second Isaiah" or Deutero-Isaiah, believed to be written by an unknown prophet who lived in Babylon during the Exile.

• Chapters 56–66 are called "Third Isaiah" or Trito-Isaiah and are attributed to a prophet (or group of prophets) who lived in Judah after the return from Babylonian Exile in 539 BCE.

The entire book depends on First Isaiah's message; the primary theme is one of consolation and hope. Isaiah assures the people that they will not be exiles forever, that God is working things out for them, if they do what they should—repent and return to God and God's ways. God is in control of history, but the people must return to God and to their covenantal obligations.

First Isaiah prophesied to Judah and Jerusalem between 742–687 BCE during the reigns of four Judean monarchs: Uzziah, Jotham, Ahaz, and Hezekiah. During this period, Judah contended with Assyria, one of the superpowers of the day. The book of Isaiah is rooted in the traditions of Moses and David—God was the great monarch of Israel and David was God's servant monarch; Jerusalem (Zion) was the city God chose to be God's royal dwelling; and monarchs of the Davidic line were to be God's servants on earth forever. Isaiah shows social injustice as evidence that Israel's relationship to God is shaky; if they lived their covenant and communal values, there would be no need for Israel to succumb to superior military and imperialist powers. Isaiah exhorts the people to put their trust in God and to live public and private lives which reflect their trust in God.

Recurring themes in Isaiah include: justice, righteousness, and assurance of divine blessing upon the faithful and divine punishment upon the unfaithful.

"Second Isaiah" is responsible for chapters 40–55, popularly called the "Book of Consolation." The prophet preached about the restoration of Israel after the Exile. The prophet's message focused on getting the people to turn back (repent) to God. This section of Isaiah is subdivided into three sections:

• Chapter 40:1–11 is the Prologue; God commissions "Second Isaiah" as a prophet during a serious convocation of the divine council. Jerusalem is in shambles and God speaks of an ideal realm of people tied to God not geographically but personally and spiritually. A new era is dawning inaugurated by God's word (just as God's word inaugurated the creation event).

• Chapters 40:12–48:22 are hymns to God the Redeemer. The prophet tells of a new creation and a new exodus initiated by Cyrus II who is being used by God for God's purposes. The creation is an ongoing process—God begins the process and God will end the process. And God can and will use every means to bring about the divine will—even the so-called enemies of Israel are part of God's plan and intention for Israel.

• Chapter 49:1–55:13 are hymns to the New Jerusalem. Jerusalem, as the city of God, is called to new greatness—the time of servitude has ended and the time of grace has come; a way in the desert has been prepared and the people will go home. The former things have passed away, and the new things that God is doing are announced—Cyrus, the Persian monarch and ruler over Israel, will expedite the restoration of Jerusalem by allowing the captives to return home; now the people will need to return to God!

In the book of Isaiah, the worst has happened—the Chosen People have experienced devastation and deportation. They have lived in foreign lands under cruel superpowers. But Exile is not God's final word for Israel—there is yet hope that Israel will once again be a great nation. First, however, Israel must stand trial for its transgression of covenantal responsibilities and duties. The fate of Israel lies in its own hands. God can only state God's case and let Israel defend itself. The prophet Isaiah is the mediator between God and God's people.

In this section of Isaiah, Israel has felt the full force of Babylon—Judah and its capital city, Jerusalem, have fallen. The unspeakable and unimaginable has happened. The nation that God called into being has been destroyed. Where was God? God had always fought Israel's battles—and now this happens? Not only is the nation destroyed but also its citizens have been deported to parts around the world. The exodus has led to exile. Israel wanted to know what the deal was and called God to answer for this calamity.

God was ready to state the divine case—the heavenly council presided over a "trial" where the plaintiff and defendant must state their cases. God began with an opening statement in Isaiah 41 outlining divine sovereignty and power—in it, God related God's relationship to the nations, to other gods, and to those who spoke for God to the heavenly council. God's opening statement rehearsed what Israel already knew—God was God! Furthermore, God testified that the "rights" of Israel had not been violated—God had rescued and delivered Israel from its enemies time and time again; God had taken care of the poor, the needy, the thirsty, and the hungry; God had used Israel's enemies to work for God's purposes and intention—all was in God's hands. If Israel was indignant, it must point fingers at itself and not at God. Israel is responsible for its own demise because it had not fully understood the relationship between nation and God; Israel had forgotten the first words of scripture, "In the beginning, God...."

And in its forgetting, Israel made unwise choices and decisions. In Israel's freedom, it now lived the consequences of those choices and decisions. God still wanted relationship and conversation. Despite the frustration of dealing with Israel, God was still willing to deal with the nation. God took Israel back to the exodus as a reminder (again) of what God had done; the reminder is also a word of assurance and hope. God was not done with Israel yet.

In our focus text, Isaiah 43:15-21, Israel is assured that God is doing a new thing. Just as God made a way back in the day, God is making a way, even now—a way more dramatic and intense than the exodus. God aims to bring Israel back to Judah and Jerusalem; the judgment is over (see Isaiah 40:1–2) and grace abounds so that the people can honor and praise God.

Why We Need This Story

Isaiah makes clear that his people have strayed from and turned their backs on God. Their worship was perfunctory and empty. They were disconnected from God, their source of life and sustenance. It would be an easy matter for God to dismiss Israel altogether and perhaps start over with a different people. But God forgives and keeps trying—God does not throw in the towel, as we might be tempted to do. Instead, God reasserts divine sovereignty and offers another chance for Israel to choose. Israel is offered new life—a new thing—that God provides. God loves Israel just that much.

The miracle is that God loves us just that much, too. Despite our ways and waywardness, God offers us new life, another chance, to choose—it is up to us to choose wisely or foolishly.

Reflection Questions

1. God sets forth the divine case (lawsuit) against Israel. What events does God recall to lay the foundations for God's case against Israel?

2. What defense can Israel make against God's allegations?

3. What picture of God emerges from this passage?

4. If you were Isaiah, what strategy would you suggest Israel follow to settle this case?

5. In what ways does the church today need to repent and return to God?

[The Holy One] has told you, O mortal, what is good;
and what does [YHWH] require of you
but to do justice, and to love kindness,
and to walk humbly with your God? (Micah 6:8)

One More Time To Get It Right...Read Amos 8:4–8

Parts of the book of Amos are often cited when we deal with social justice issues. His prophecies are strident indictments against the rich and powerful. His message is uncompromising—God's judgment will be the result of the people's acts of social injustice and religious arrogance.

Amos prophesied during the reigns of two monarchs: Uzziah of Judah and Jeroboam II of Israel. Although a native of Judah (Southern Kingdom; he hailed from Tekoa, in the hills south of Bethlehem), Amos preached to Israel (the Northern Kingdom; in the major cities of Samaria and Bethel) during a time of economic prosperity and military security. There were no major military threats and a small number of Israelites were doing quite well financially. But Israel's reliance on its military prowess, its shaky economic practices, and its superficial piety would only lead to its downfall.

For Amos, justice means doing the right things for the right reasons. Righteousness is living in ways that honor members of the community. The covenant means that persons live according to the teachings of the Torah; anything else is a breach of contract and will bring judgment. Amos' challenge was preaching a message of justice during a period of ease and comfort; he had the task of shaking up the people enough for them to hear the message he brought from God.

In our Bible study text, Amos spells out in graphic detail the corrupt practices of grain tycoons, in league with the temple bankers, who tamper with the very life of the economy—the weights and measures, and the valuation of money. Through unjust economic practices, the poor are being exterminated. The traditional days of religious observance and rest are merely tolerated by the merchants who resent these interruptions to their profit-making. The rich get richer and the poor get poorer. Amos calls for a radical union of ethics and religion—walk the walk and talk the talk according to the teachings of the Torah.

Amos condemns the monarchs who rely on military expertise; and he condemns the priests who make a mockery of worship by merely going through the motions. Amos challenges the Israelites to get back on track and renew their covenant with God before it's too late. His warning was unheeded and nearly forty years after his ministry, Israel was defeated by Assyria.

Why We Need This Story

It is not difficult to see why suffering people love the book of Amos. The prophet pulls no punches—he exposes the brutality of greed and the emptiness of words. For Amos, true believers live what they profess. His words were appropriate for his situation—the poor were exploited, even among his kinfolk. Those who had wealth and status disregarded the worth and humanity of the less fortunate. His words ring vividly today, because Amos' socio-economic and political context is so close to our own. The words of prophecy are not just relevant to an age long gone; they are all too relevant for our contemporary context. Governments around the globe engage in practices that benefit a few while the masses are poor, hungry, and homeless. Modern day prophets echo the words of Amos—God is displeased with the ways in which we treat the least among us. The call to social justice will reverberate down the years—John the Baptist, Jesus, Paul, Gandhi, Martin Luther King, Jr., Shirley Chisholm, Barbara Jordan, Bill Moyers, Marian Wright Edelman—all speak words of truth to power. All lift up the prophetic words in their speeches and prayers:

> *...let justice roll down like waters,*
> *and righteousness like an ever-flowing stream.* (Amos 5:24.)

Reflection Questions

1. If Amos lived today, to whom would he address his message? Explain your answer.

2. What picture of God emerges from this passage?

3. Amos preached during a time of stability; how do you think people reacted to his message?

4. How would you preach a message of justice and righteousness to the rich and powerful of our day?

5. Who are the modern versions of Amos today? Explain your choices.

Eight

The Writings

But Ruth said,
"Do not press me to leave you
or to turn back from following you!
Where you go, I will go;
where you lodge, I will lodge;
your people shall be my people,
and your God my God.
Where you die, I will die –
there will I be buried.
May [YHWH] do thus and so to me,
and more as well,
if even death parts me from you!" (Ruth 1:16–17)

The last of the three major divisions of the Hebrew Bible is called "The Writings" (in Hebrew, *ketubim*). It includes works of "history" (Chronicles, Ezra, Nehemiah); hymnody (Psalms, Lamentations, Song of Songs); learned wisdom (Proverbs, Ecclesiastes); and a collection of stories (Job, Ruth, Esther, Daniel).

The first division of the Hebrew Bible, Torah, is the revealed "constitution" of Israel as the covenant people of God. The second division, Former and Latter Prophets, documents the history of the covenant relationship from the period of the initial conquest under Joshua through the early phases of Judean restoration after a period of exile; it is the prophetic witness to the on-going importance of the divinely-given Torah. Together, Torah and Prophets establish Israel's fundamental identity as God's creation and establish the standard for the spiritual, ritual and ethical discipline by which this identity must be lived.

The Writings deal with the life of faith. This faith is manifested in praise of God, confronts doubt, searches for understanding, and maintains faith under the pressure of adversity. The Writings are made up of songs, prayers, collections of wise sayings and stories.

"Wisdom" literature is a modern critical term to describe literary works found in other places in the ancient Near East. The central unit of this literature in the Bible is the proverb (in Hebrew, *mashal*), a two-part sentence that highlights some essential truth about life. The *mashal* is the basic building block for the books of Job, Proverbs, and Ecclesiastes.

"Wisdom" was a class of writings in ancient Israel; it was viewed as a way to life, a way of life, and a way of understanding the world. The sage, or wise one, looked deeply into the meaning of things. The sage was also one (like Joseph and Daniel) who interpreted dreams and other mysteries.

The basic assumption of the world of wisdom was that the world made sense and that, underlying the confusion, injustice, and disorder of daily life, there was a pattern, an order by which everything could be understood. This pattern is sometimes called "wisdom" (in Hebrew, *hokmah*) as in Proverbs 3:19:

> By wisdom [YHWH] founded the earth;
> by understanding [God] established the heavens.

An important virtue in wisdom was patience. Only with patience could one avoid hasty judgments and escape the prison of the moment. Patience meant the ability to wait things out *and* the ability to accept discomfort and suffering. The sage was one who believed that things would be all right no matter what was happening at the moment.

The virtue of patience is seen in the book of Proverbs, a collection of wise sayings and exhortations from different time periods and geographical settings. The qualities of honesty, diligence, self-control and humility are praised and their opposites are condemned. Wisdom, then, is associated with older folks rather than with youth who are seen as impetuous, impulsive, and immature. The older person is one who knows the lessons of the past and one who has endured!

The Jewish canonical tradition divides the Writings listed below:

- "the books of Truth" (in Hebrew, *emet*): Psalms, Job, Proverbs
- "[Five] scrolls" (in Hebrew, *megillot*): Song of Songs, Ruth, Ecclesiastes, Lamentations, Esther
- Others: Daniel, Ezra, Nehemiah and Chronicles

For everything there is a season, and a time for every matter under heaven:
a time to be born, and a time to die;
a time to plant, and a time to pluck up what is planted;
a time to kill, and a time to heal;
a time to break down, and a time to build up;
a time to weep, and a time to laugh;
a time to mourn, and a time to dance;
a time to throw away stones, and a time to gather stones together;
a time to embrace, and a time to refrain from embracing;
a time to seek, and a time to lose;
a time to keep, and a time to throw away;
a time to tear, and a time to sew;
a time to keep silence, and a time to speak;
a time to love, and a time to hate;
a time for war, and a time for peace. (Ecclesiastes 3:1-8.)

What's the Point of Worshipping God...Read Job 2:1-13

In popular culture, Job is considered the exemplar of the patient person. However, the Book of Job does *not* attempt to explain the mystery of suffering or to justify the ways of God to humankind. Instead, it aims at probing the depths of faith in spite of suffering! Job is a prime example of wisdom literature. It is like the simple stories that also circulated in Canaanite religious traditions. In these stories, the gods were divine and ruled the world in which humans were the subjects. These gods acted arbitrarily at times and were seen as divine parents; humans were devotees who needed to be guided and nurtured.

The Book of Job is a mixture of poetry and prose, and its author is unknown. The story evokes memories of faithful heroes like Noah and Daniel. It points to the late sixth or fifth century BCE because of its focus on monotheism and monogamous marriage. Job's story is one that starts in riches, moves to rags, and returns to riches. Job seems to be a pawn in a conversation between God and "Satan" (see Job. 1:1–19). The Hebrew word translated "Satan" is *hassatan*, a generic word meaning "accuser" or "adversary." In the context of this passage, "Satan" is *not* God's equal nor the "devil" found in later Jewish and Christian works. "Satan" is not the embodiment of evil we read about in John Milton's *Paradise Lost*. In the Book of Job, "Satan" has the job of asking questions and contesting the status quo. "Satan" challenges God's assumptions and assessments of human beings, especially Job himself. "Satan" asks important questions about the integrity of humans in matters of faith and fidelity.

The Book of Job addresses the theological question of theodicy, which examines the meaning of undeserved suffering before the silence and inactivity of God. What is one to make of the tradition, of oneself, and of the divine character and purpose in view of such experience? These questions assumed a connection between human piety and divine action. Job's friends, as did others of those times, believed that people were rewarded for being good and punished for being bad. Job's experience called this into question. Job displayed covenantal loyalty and continued to address God as God! God spoke directly to Job; Job affirmed monotheism as well as the transcendence of the God of Israel.

The Book of Job deals with the theological issue of justice: (a) for the oppressed and helpless, justice is liberation and salvation; and (b) for the disobedient and disloyal, justice is destruction. Wisdom taught the efficacy of righteous living; it tried to reduce the arbitrary and unpredicted elements in life. God had revealed instructions (the teachings of the Torah) that governed life; these instructions can be known and followed for a life of harmony, happiness, and success. Wisdom dealt with real life as opposed to an ideal life.

Job's wife asks the poignant question—why bother with God at all? Job's friends asked the same question in different ways as they tried to understand how it was that Job, a righteous and upright man, had lost everything and suffered physically. Job's wife asked the question that everyone was thinking; it's the same question that Job himself eventually poses to God. It is a question that many people wrestle with today. It is a question that challenges believers—it is good to spend some time reflecting on the question.

Job's answer to his wife suggests that God may have purposes other than retributive justice. That is, perhaps God is not keeping a tally of rewards for good deeds and punishment for bad ones. Eliphaz, Bildad and Zophar, Job's friends, were eloquent defenders of the "traditional" understanding of faith and life—the good prosper and the bad suffer. Their positive doctrine was sound and helpful but they refused to admit the limits to their understanding. They had fallen into the occupational hazard of some theologians, even today—they forgot that they were dealing with mystery.

In his heart, Job knew he had done nothing to deserve the catastrophe that had befallen him. Although he was able to give thoughtful responses to his wife and to his three friends, he still pondered the question. Job's confrontation with God is an interesting one. Job has serious doubts about God's power and authority—where was God when Job needed him most? At the same time, Job did not want to totally abandon his trust and belief in a good and gracious God.

Job learned that the question was not, "Why do bad things happen to good people?" Instead, the question was, "How is the believer to respond when bad things happen?" Job dared to ask God about God's motives, power, and compassion for humans. God provided a catalog of divine deeds and asked Job what he had done that was comparable. Job realized that he was dealing with mystery—that he would never understand the ways of God. Instead, Job was left with the assurance that God was in charge of the cosmos and all things happened with God's sanction. Job learned that bad things happen, but God did not abandon him. Although God was not apparent, God was still there, working to bring Job into a deeper understanding of life and faith—read Job 42:1–6.

Why We Need this Story

If the Garden incident in Genesis 3 has been strangely interpreted and the Decalogue in Exodus 20 has been widely quoted, then the Book of Job has a share, too. The Book of Job shapes our understanding of the "good" life—mostly based on social status and economic stability. When a person says, "I'm blessed!" most often he refers to the material aspects of life. There has always been a sector of Christianity focused on material prosperity and this sector seems to be growing in recent years. While God and the prophets are concerned about socio-economic and political well-being, it is never in the service of a few individuals. God's concern is with community—how are we to live so that every member of the community has what is needed. Any other message is short-sighted.

For some, the Book of Job is "proof" that God means to bless us with riches. Job's life is restored, bigger and better than before. However, the point of Job's saga is not his material gains. Rather, the point is about how people of faith live their lives. We live knowing that no matter what, God is faithful. Even when God is silent and seemingly absent, we live with the hope and assurance that God is working things out according to God's purposes and intentions.

Into each life, some rain will fall—there will be ups and downs, bad things will happen to good people and good things will happen to bad people—that's the human condition. But we live in the hope that God is alive and always working for our good. Our true character emerges when we are in a crisis. Too many of us question God when adversity strikes. Too often we try to bargain with God: "If you just get me out of this jam, I promise to be good." Too many of our prayers ask God to undo something already in progress. We invest our security in our capacity to do the right things.

Job's story takes us deeper into what faith is—certainly, family, health, and financial well-being are important. There is no denying that. And the loss of any one of them hurts—the pain is real as are all the emotions that attend any loss. But Job understands that everything that happens in life is within the scope of God's care and concern. Job understands that good and bad things happen—but they don't determine God's presence and care. And this is the lesson of wisdom: God is always near, searching for us, seeking us out. Just when it seems that God has forsaken and abandoned us, God shows up. A saying that holds meaning for me is one I've heard most of my life, "God may not come when we want, but God is always on time!" We can depend on God—no matter what!

Reflection Questions

1. What image of God emerges from this passage? Explain your answer.

2. God does not cause Job's suffering, but allows it. How do you explain evil, undeserved suffering, and oppression?

3. What lessons have you learned from Job's story to help you deal with difficult times and hardships?

4. "Satan" is a member of God's heavenly assembly. How does this change your understanding of evil and the devil?

5. Has your faith ever been tested? Share as much as you feel comfortable.

Where can I go from your spirit?
Or where can I flee from your presence?
If I ascend to heaven, you are there;
if I make my bed in Sheol, you are there. (Psalm 139:7–8.)

A Very Present Help in the Time of Need...Read Psalm 23

The Book of Psalms, or Psalter, is a collection of 150 compositions that are generally described as praises and prayers addressed to God. The Psalms (in Hebrew, *tehillim*, meaning "hymns" or "songs of praise") are diverse. Many were connected with the formal worship conducted at special sacred sites like the Temple at Jerusalem. The offering of sacrifices and of songs were two aspects of worship: sacrifices were the tangible way that people communicated with God and songs and prayers were a more poetic, verbal, emotional way.

While many of the psalms are prayers and praise; some are expressions of communal celebration; some evoke states of distress such as illness or personal problems; and others offer thanksgiving to God for having heard one's cry in the time of need. Since ancient times, the Book of Psalms has been the foundation for Jewish and Christian spirituality, providing actual liturgies for synagogues and churches as well as serving as the foundation for hymns and songs. The reciting of psalms as a form of individual devotion has flourished since ancient times, also.

The major types of psalms include:

• hymns or acts of praise suitable for any occasion; subtypes are the enthronement hymns that celebrated God's sovereignty and songs of Zion expressing devotion to the Holy City

• laments by which an individual seeks deliverance from illness or false accusation or a nation asks for help in time of distress

• songs of trust in which an individual expresses confidence in God's readiness to help

• songs of thanksgiving in which an individual expresses gratitude for deliverance

• songs of sacred history in which a nation recounts the story of God's dealings with it

• royal psalms that were used at occasions like coronations or royal weddings

• wisdom psalms that served as meditations on life and the ways of God

• liturgies that were composed for some special religious or historical occasion, like the annual ceremony for renewing the covenant.

Some individual prayers and songs were used in communal settings just as some communal psalms were used by individuals. The psalms deal with issues of sickness, adversity, betrayal, abandonment, sin, guilt, slander, persecution, oppression, and joy. The theological focus of the psalms is that God is creator *and* savior. The psalms generally highlight the character of God as well as the confidence of the believer in a God who cares and acts on behalf of the believer.

Scholars are not able to neither date the psalms nor identify authors with certainty. Many are attributed to David who was known to be a musician and could have composed hymns and songs. Some were composed early in Israel's history and others likely after the Exile. In its present form, the Book of Psalms is divided into five collections:

- Book I: Psalms 1–41
- Book II: Psalms 42–72
- Book III: Psalms 73–89
- Book IV: Psalms 90–106
- Book V: Psalms 107–150

Try to read Psalm 23 in different translations to get a feel for its poetry and pathos. Psalm 23 is a familiar song—it speaks of confidence in God who is compassionate and strong. The image of God as shepherd and people as flock is developed here—see Ezekiel 34:11, Isaiah 40:11, John 10:11,14. This Psalm exhibits complete trust and confidence in God. Verse 4 speaks of situations of the most terrifying distress or suffering. The rod is a club used to keep wild animals away; the staff is a long stick used to keep sheep from wandering off. Ancient Israel developed a custom of anointing honored guests with oil. Finally, one is pursued by God's goodness and mercy just as one had been pursued by one's enemies.

Why We Need this Story

Psalm 23 is a precious passage of scripture. It is among the first passages many are taught and among the first many memorize. It is a psalm of comfort and assurance. It is the foundation for a great many religious works of art—Sunday school resources have some depiction of this psalm. I use this psalm as a reminder to those going through a trial—illness, setbacks, or emotional distress—that God is present. My words are simple, "You walk *through* the valley, you don't stay there! And as you walk, God is there leading you through and out of the valley!" This is one of my favorite psalms; another favorite is

Psalm 139. Both speak of a God who is "so high, I can't get over; so low, I can't get under; so wide, I can't get around!" What a wonderful God we serve.

Reflection Questions

1. What differences do you note in the various translations of Psalm 23? What do the differences convey?

2. What picture of God emerges from this psalm?

3. In what ways would people of color read this psalm? Explain your answer.

4. What does it mean to be part of God's flock?

5. What is your favorite psalm? Why does it hold meaning for you?

Nine

Intertestamental Concerns

*See, I am sending my messenger to prepare the way before me, and
the Lord whom you seek will suddenly come to his temple. The messenger
of the covenant in whom you delight—indeed, he is coming, says
[YHWH] of hosts. But who can endure the day of his coming, and who
can stand when he appears?* (Malachi 3:1–2.)

Before we shift to New Testament writings, let's spend a little time filling in information of Israel's life after the Exile. Here, we rely on the
books of 1 and 2 Chronicles, Ezra, and Nehemiah for information. The
Chronicler accepts the Deuteronomistic view that the Exile was the result of
national sin and found sufficient reason for the disaster in Judah. Note that
the issue of infidelity, sin, and unfaithfulness was not based on individual
piety or lack thereof, but rested on the people collectively. Therefore, any
deliverance, rescue, or salvation would be for the community. Theologically,
1 and 2 Chronicles declared that there was a need for a worship life that was
beautiful, vocal and based on the foundational traditions of Moses. There was
to be an ideal of social justice undergirding the community and society.

At one time, Ezra and Nehemiah comprised one book. It is generally accepted that Ezra was written by the Chronicler (or, at least in that tradition)
and serves as a supplement to 1 and 2 Chronicles on the basis of Hebrew and

Aramaic documents, memoirs of Nehemiah, a memorial to Ezra, genealogies and archives. Second Chronicles ends with the destruction of Jerusalem and the deportation of captives and treasures throughout the Babylonian Empire. Persia rose to be a world power. Persian rulers allowed some of their Jewish captives to return to Jerusalem. Ezra tells how some returned to reestablish life and religion in Jerusalem. The exiles developed their religion because it was their bond of unity; without religion, they would have lost the sense of what it meant to be Jewish. They had to hold on to their faith as they adjusted to life outside of Jerusalem. This was *not* the case for folks who remained in Jerusalem.

The religion of the exiles placed emphasis on the laws associated with Moses. When the exiles returned to Jerusalem, they were concerned with rebuilding the altar, the Temple, and the city as well as dealing with social and religious problems, freeing the community of foreign elements and establishing religious practices in stricter conformity to Mosaic law as they understood it. The returned exiles were the godly remnant with a religious mission.

There were four stages of the return from exile:

• some returned under Cyrus led by Sheshbazzar, who began rebuilding the Temple but left it undone because of local opposition around 538 BCE

• some returned under Darius I, led by Zerubbabel and Jeshua who were encouraged by Haggai and Zechariah and completed the Temple

• some comprised a group led by Nehemiah who came twice under Artaxerxes I to rebuild the walls of Jerusalem and attempt to establish purity of community and worship

• some returned under Artaxerxes II, led by Ezra who codified Mosaic law and found a community relapsing to old idolatrous ways.

The exiles returned to Jerusalem but the great renewal that the prophets preached did not occur. The Temple had been rebuilt, but there was no Davidic golden age. After Persia succumbed to Greece, Israel experienced more ups and downs. The Persians had been willing to extend some liberties towards the exiled Jews that included the practice of their religion. Alexander the Great tried to unite his vast empire by making everyone conform to the same language and religion. After his death, his generals took turns at leadership; early on, Jews were allowed to maintain their customs and religion. But when Antiochus IV Epiphanes rose to power, he wanted the Jews to conform to Greek ways and customs. He destroyed written copies of Jewish scriptures; he outlawed religious practices such as circumcision and observance of the

Sabbath; and he set up an image of Zeus in the temple. While most Jews were outraged and offended, few did anything about it except for Mattathias Maccabeus and his five sons. They rebelled against Antiochus from 166–142 BCE. The Maccabean Revolt restored a bit of normalcy to Jewish life; the temple was cleansed and rededicated. But their reprieve was short-lived.

Rome became the dominant world power and soon took Jerusalem. The priests were assassinated and the temple defiled again. The next few years were dominated by some familiar folks—Julius Caesar, Cleopatra, and Mark Antony, to name a few. Rome established government representatives in the Middle East, including Jerusalem. The various leaders allowed some freedom, but as you can imagine, most Jews were not happy campers.

The people splintered into various groups and movements for religious, political and social reasons. Some wanted a return to the glory and power days of David and Solomon. Some wanted to renew the Mosaic covenant and live by the teachings of the Torah. Some felt the best way was to assimilate to whatever power was dominant at the time. A few of the prominent groups mentioned in the New Testament include:

• The **Pharisees** were the primary interpreters of Mosaic teachings, including observance of the Sabbath, purification rituals, and food restrictions. They tried to implement a comprehensive and coherent plan of religious reform which focused on living holy and righteous lives as a way to reclaim their position as God's chosen people. Modern Judaism traces its roots back to the reform movement of the Pharisees. Most Pharisees were laypeople, although some were priests and others sat on the Sanhedrin, the religious council of elders and leaders. Leaders of the Pharisees were called rabbis or teachers and scribes. Pharisees believed in the resurrection of the dead and the Apostle Paul was a Pharisee. The Pharisees and Christians parted ways when Paul and others started teaching Jesus in the synagogues.

• The **Sadducees** were influential though smaller in numbers than the Pharisees. The Sadducees were an elite and priestly class of Jews who embraced the Torah only. They worked hard to maintain their privileged position and were unpopular with ordinary Jews. They were closely associated with the temple and the ruling council, the Sanhedrin. They did not believe in the resurrection of the dead. They are portrayed as opponents of Jesus in the Gospels.

• The **Essenes** were Jews who lived a monastic life at Qumran (near the Dead Sea) during the time the Pharisees and Sadducees were forming. They are responsible for the preservation of the Dead Sea Scrolls (copies of the

Hebrew Bible, some non-canonical texts, and writings indigenous to their community) found in the mid-1940s. They were originally a group of priests and felt the best way to live the teachings of the Torah was to separate themselves from corrupting influences. It is likely that John the Baptist knew of the Essenes because he lived, preached, taught, and baptized a few miles from their community. They did not believe in the resurrection of the dead. The Essenes are not mentioned in the New Testament but the Jewish historian, Josephus, mentions them.

• The **Zealots** were Jewish nationalists who were strongly opposed to the Roman Empire. They were active during the first century CE. It is important to note, however, that there were numerous revolutionary groups active in the early years of the Christian movement. In 66 CE, the Zealots captured the temple in Jerusalem but then were soundly defeated by Roman forces. They were effectively wiped out at Masada (a wilderness stronghold near the Dead Sea) shortly after 70 CE.

• The **Samaritans** were not considered to be Israelites by Jews in Jerusalem and Judah. The hostility between Jews and Samaritans is traced back to the political split of the nation Israel after Solomon's death. The Samaritans believed the Torah to be the only scripture, but worshiped at Mount Gerizim rather than Jerusalem. First and Second Chronicles focus on the hatred between the Jews and Samaritans. It was felt that Israel, the Northern Kingdom, did not represent the "True Israel" because God had promised an eternal dynasty to David. The Samaritans traced their roots back to tribes of Manasseh and Ephraim (Joseph's sons). The Chronicler's hostility to the Northern Kingdom is sometimes attributed to the hatred of Samaritans that we will see in the Gospels. The Samaritans gained influence with the Romans by fighting against the Zealots. During Jesus' day, Herod, monarch of the Jews, lived in a Samaritan city and married a Samaritan woman. Jesus' parable of the "good Samaritan" would have been a shocking turn of events for those in Jerusalem; the Samaritans were their bitter enemy and to have a Samaritan as the hero of a story would have offended a good number of Jews.

• **Scribes** were Jews who studied the Torah and were important interpreters and teachers of the Torah. They were responsible for legal documents, land deeds, copying the scripture, and teaching. They did not form a separate group. Most scribes were Pharisees and in the Gospels the two names are often linked.

• The **Herodians** were probably a small group that supported Herod, especially Herod Antipas who ruled over Galilee during the time of Jesus and John the Baptist. They are only mentioned in the Gospel of Mark and Matthew.

• **Priests** and **Levites**, along with the High Priest and other priests, were members of the tribe of Levi who took care of the temple and worship life. They had social and religious influence. The High Priest was appointed each year; during Jesus' time, the High Priest was Annas whose son, Caiaphas, succeeded him. The chief priests are depicted as opponents of Jesus who co-operated with the Roman authorities to have Jesus crucified.

• The **publicans** were professional tax collectors—they made profits by extorting more than was owed in taxes and pocketing the difference. They did not form a specific group, but were Jews who were ostracized and hated by other Jews because they exploited their own kin. Some came to believe in Jesus and joined his movement.

There were a number of other groups active as the days of the Hebrew Bible closed and the days of the New Testament began. It is important to note that a period of about 400 years separates the Hebrew Bible and the early days of the New Testament. In between were times of relative rest and times of violent domination and rebellion. The Jews struggled to maintain some sense of identity and religion in the face of great odds. What happened to the new thing God had promised Isaiah?

The Hebrew Bible ends its prophetic section with the Book of Malachi. The closing words of Malachi refer to Elijah's return that will herald God's final judgment. For Jews, the expectation of the Messiah lingers. For Christians, God does a new thing in Jesus of Nazareth.

Reflection Questions

1. What kind of "messiah" did the Jews long for during biblical times?

2. What do you think God was up to in the 400 years after the close of the Hebrew Bible?

3. Isaiah's prophecy of a new thing seemed unfulfilled. How do you think the people reacted to his prophecy?

4. What happens to hope that seems delayed or denied?

Ten

The Gospels

In those days Jesus came from Nazareth of Galilee and was baptized by John in the Jordan. And just as he was coming up out of the water, he saw the heavens torn apart and the Spirit descending like a dove on him. And a voice came from heaven, "You are my Son, the Beloved; with you I am well pleased." (Mark 1:9–11.)

Gospel" is from a Greek word that means "good news." The secular use of the word included announcements—weddings, births, military triumphs, etc. Before the mid-second century CE, gospel referred to the oral tradition that highlighted God's new thing—salvation and deliverance through Jesus. Justin Martyr and Irenaeus coined the term to refer to a literary genre. It is widely agreed that the Gospel of Mark provides the basic outline for the Synoptic Gospels; Mark is the source of information for Matthew and Luke. However, Matthew and Luke share material not found in Mark and each has material unique to itself. These sources are unrecoverable and are designated as "M" for Matthew's extra material, "L" for Luke's extra material, and "Q" (German *Quelle* meaning "source") for material that Matthew and Luke share that is not in Mark. "Q" is believed to be a collection of sayings and teachings of Jesus. It is believed that these materials are bits of oral and written traditions that were in circulation shortly after the resurrection but before the writing of the gospels.

Each gospel has a unique perspective on the Christ event and grows out of concerns dominant in those communities that produced it. A brief overview of the gospels follows:

• Matthew, believed to be a Greek-speaking Israelite, connects the gospel story with God's saving acts in the Hebrew Bible (Matthew opens with a lengthy genealogy that links Jesus back to Abraham and to David). Matthew wants to show that Jesus is God's fulfillment promised in the Torah and the prophets, and that the church is a continuation of God's ongoing work of redemption. Matthew is the only Gospel that speaks of the "church" as the community of believers. Matthew speaks to a Jewish Christian audience as well as to Gentiles. The leading religious leaders are called the Pharisees; their responsibility was that of keeping the Jewish faith and downplaying the Christian movement. Matthew's community was deeply involved in trying to show how Jesus was God's Messiah, long anticipated by the people of Israel. Matthew saw his community in a waiting period where they must be missionaries (see Matthew 28:19–20) until Jesus returned to claim his church. The Gospel is dated late first century, perhaps 90 CE.

• Mark's is the earliest written account of the Jesus story. He intends for his work to be a "gospel" (see Mark 1:1). Jesus is the "Son of God" and the cross is the key to understanding Jesus' identity and his purposes. Mark's audience is primarily Gentile; his community's suffering at the hands of the Roman government and the Jewish leaders of the synagogue mirrors the suffering of Jesus during his passion. Mark's agenda reflects more a historical than a biographical concern. God has intervened, once again, in history to redeem the time and to redeem God's people. The Gospel dates from around 65–70 CE.

• Luke purports to write a more objective story about Jesus and his works (see Luke 1:1–4). This gospel is more "historical" than the others, in that Luke includes the names and dates of persons found in works outside the Bible. Luke also includes information about the early church in his two-volume work (the Gospel of Luke and the Book of Acts). Jesus is the Messiah who ushers in God's new world order that is radically inclusive—Luke talks a great deal about outcasts, women, and sinners who are included in Jesus' sphere of forgiveness and fellowship. The date is difficult to pinpoint—somewhere around 70–90 CE, probably mid-80s.

• John continues to generate a great deal of scholarly debate about authorship and date. About the most we can say with certainty is that a Jewish

Christian whose community had been cast out of the synagogue composed the Gospel. John's gospel is different enough from Matthew, Mark and Luke to be labeled "Asynoptic." John's book is filled with different images and symbols as it tells the story of Jesus. Instead of the short moral teachings (parables) and instructions that we find in the Synoptics, John shows Jesus speaking in long discourses and having long debates with his opponents. Most of the discourses and debates address the validity of Jesus' messiahship and relationship to God. Jesus' words serve to confuse people, even his disciples, and he is often misunderstood. There are many references to Hebrew scripture and John uses dualities or contrasts (light and shadows; belief and doubt; life and death) to express the meaning of the Jesus event. John's mission is to persuade people that Jesus is God's Chosen One and God's fulfillment to bring eternal life to the world. A likely date for the gospel is 100 CE.

The New Testament gospels resemble the ancient Hellenistic biography—in these works, there is a hero who has human and divine origins, who exhibits special gifts, and who dies an unusual death. While the gospels are not strictly biographies, they are the memories of communities who found value in the stories about Jesus. Just as God acted in history for the Israelites, God continued to act in history. The formative events of exodus and exile now give way to God's work through Jesus of Nazareth. Despite the wide diversity of oral traditions that make up the New Testament, the central figure is Jesus and God's work through him gave birth to a new religion, Christianity. There are now millions of Christians all over the world who express their faith in diverse ways but they all revolve around the person of Jesus who stood in the legacy of Moses and was identified as the promised messianic monarch for whom Israel had been waiting.

The New Testament stands as a witness that God had not abandoned Israel. In the New Testament, God is fulfilling the divine promise of a "new thing" that the prophets envisioned. God breaks the divine silence when John the Baptist heralds the imminent arrival of God's Anointed One. Remember that Israel lived with the expectation that God would intervene once more in its history and work miracles. The people expected a deliverer on the order of Moses and David. For some, this expectation was wrapped in a revolutionary and military action.

When Jesus emerges as a personality, there is some concern about whether he is the One sent by God. Jesus enters the world under quite modest circumstances—there are questions about his paternity and identity.

He begins his ministry after being baptized by John the Baptist, a popular teacher but a quirky personality. Jesus is able to do incredible things—giving sight to the blind, helping the lame to walk, feeding massive numbers of people with few resources, raising the dead, providing new insights to ancient lessons—all the while talking about a new realm, the Realm of God, that is inclusive, open, peaceful, and loving. Many believed that Jesus was God's Messiah—how else could they explain his power and his insight? Others thought he was a forerunner of the Messiah; they believed Jesus was a reincarnated Elijah or Moses or some other prophet. But they had a hard time believing that this humble carpenter from Galilee could be sent by God. Still others believed Jesus was a false prophet, leading the people astray.

There were a number of teachers in those days and the religious authorities had the task of weeding out the charlatans from the authentic teachers. The Sanhedrin, a group of influential Jews that included religious and possibly political leaders, was responsible for interpreting Jewish life, customs, and faith. The New Testament does not specify who the members of the council were nor does it state their specific duties. Some of them didn't give much thought to Jesus; others thought Jesus should be silenced. In the days of the early church, the Sanhedrin judged the preaching of Peter and John (see Acts 4).

Through an amazing series of events—Jesus called a number of persons to follow him, Jesus taught and trained men and women to do the work of God, Jesus debated with religious authorities, Jesus worked wonders and miracles, Jesus entered Jerusalem at the Passover to a roaring crowd, Jesus hosted a solemn last supper with his disciples where he predicted his demise, Jesus was betrayed by one of his disciples, Jesus stood trial before the religious and political leaders of Jerusalem, Jesus was crucified along with two thieves, Jesus died after uttering a number of words, and Jesus was laid in a borrowed tomb—Jesus, revolutionary, healer, teacher, and all-around good guy was executed by Roman authorities. This should have been the end of the story—God had fooled the people and Jesus was no Messiah. On that horrible Good Friday, the disciples and other followers of Jesus walked away from Golgotha, scared, depressed, disillusioned, and disappointed. Their hopes for a new world order had died on a rugged cross on a hill with common thieves.

And that would have been the end of the story. But some women went to the tomb to anoint the body with spices and to complete the proper burial rituals—but Jesus' body was missing. Various theories circulated about what could have happened to Jesus. His followers believed that God had raised him from death—see Matthew 28: 1–20; Mark 16:1–8; Luke 24:1–12; John 20:1–18. The first "Christian" preachers were women—Mary Magdalene the primary evangelist! Jesus appeared to his disciples, gave them missionary instructions, and planted the seeds for what would become a new religion.

▼ ▼ ▼

The people who walked in darkness
have seen a great light;
those who lived in a land of deep darkness—
on them light has shined. Isaiah 9:2

It's Not Over Until It's Over...Read Matthew 1:1–25

The Gospel of Matthew was composed by a subject of the Roman Empire—he speaks of a hierarchal social order—wealthy landowners, government bureaucrats, slaves, priests, military personnel, local businesspeople, artisans, farmers and fisher folk. The outsiders included lepers, bandits, and beggars. There are tensions in the Matthean community between those who believe Jesus is God's new thing and those who don't. Many do not see Jesus as God's Messiah, the promised redeemer of Israel; Jesus may be a good person, but he was not God's Anointed One. In Matthew, Jesus speaks on behalf of the poor and is in constant tension with both Jewish and Roman authorities. Jesus' primary religious opponents are depicted as the Pharisees (see Mt 9:11, 34; 12:2; 27:62).

The hostility in Matthew's gospel between Jesus and the Pharisees actually reflects tensions that occurred after Jesus' time. During his life and shortly after the resurrection, followers of Jesus were seen as a sect of Judaism. It took a while for the Christian communities to establish their identity apart from their Jewish ancestors. At the same time that the Christian communities were forming, Judaism was in the process of solidifying its own identity in the wake of the destruction of the Second Temple in 70 CE. Much of what we find in Matthew is a reflection of the tension between the early churches and the synagogues, and not that between Jesus and the Pharisees.

Matthew's gospel follows the geographical outline of Mark from Galilee to Jerusalem. Matthew brackets this outline with birth stories at the beginning and resurrection and commissioning stories at the end. Jesus is portrayed as the new Moses offering a new Torah that fulfills the old but does not eliminate it. Matthew wants to prove that Jesus stands in the legacy of Abraham, Moses, and David and that Jesus is God's Anointed One or Messiah.

The Gospel of Matthew opens with a lengthy genealogy of Jesus' family. Jesus' family tree begins with Abraham and ends with Joseph. Note that Joseph is referred to as the "husband of Mary"—in most ancient writings, men are identified by their fathers, not their wives! Mary, the mother of Jesus, is used by God to do a new thing. She accepts God's invitation and Joseph goes along with the program. In Hebrew, "Jesus" is *yasha*, which means "he saves;" it was a common name. In verse 23, the word translated "virgin" is based on a Hebrew word *(almah)* which is usually translated "young woman." When Joseph names the child Jesus, he indicates his acceptance of the child as his own. The text indicates that Mary goes on to have other children.

Why We Need this Story

This passage serves as a bridge between the Old and New Testaments. The Hebrew Bible clearly establishes Israel as God's Chosen People. The Jews are chosen to be a light to the nations. Although they failed to live up to God's high expectations, they find that God continues to search for them.

The appearance of Jesus heralds the new thing God promised. Everyone knows something about Christmas. It's even on the calendar as a national holiday in the United States. Folks who practice other religions are held captive by the Christmas story. Jesus' birth is the reason for the season and for a multitude of art forms, literature and music. The "Christmas" season is marked by all sorts of secular activity: decorations of all types, colorful clothing, shopping splurges (after all, Christmas only comes once a year!), mysterious rituals (mistletoe, eggnog, roasted chestnuts, chimney visitations), and a surge of movies. The country is captivated by the religious, secular, and economic aspects of what was intended to be a holy day.

So much of what we know about Christmas is colored by cultural interpretations of the biblical story. The truth is that while some rejoiced at the birth of Jesus, others lived in fear. Herod the Great, the ruler of the Jews, was so terrified that he ordered all boys two years old and younger to be slaughtered. The mere threat to his power by an infant led him to this brutal act (see Matthew 2:1–18). As we will see, Jesus' presence is like a double-edged sword—for some, he brings great joy; and for others, he brings great distress. God is definitely up to something!

Reflection Questions

1. What message is Matthew conveying by listing four women, Tamar, Rahab, Ruth, and Bathsheba (the wife of Uriah), in Jesus' genealogy? What is the significance of listing four women of questionable virtue?

2. Why is it important to list the monarchs of Judah in verses 6–11? What is Matthew establishing by this list?

3. Christian tradition indicates that Jesus was born to Mary, who was a virgin. What does the tradition want to convey by talking about Jesus' birth in this manner?

4. What kind of man is Joseph in this passage? Explain your answer.

> When [Jesus] came to Nazareth, where he had been brought up,
> he went to the synagogue on the sabbath day, as was his custom.
> He stood up to read, and the scroll of the prophet Isaiah was given to
> him. He unrolled the scroll and found the place where it was written:
> "The Spirit of the Lord is upon me,
> because he has anointed me
> to bring good news to the poor.
> He has sent me to proclaim release to the captives
> and recovery of sight to the blind,
> to let the oppressed go free,
> to proclaim the year of the Lord's favor."
> And he rolled up the scroll, gave it back to the attendant,
> and sat down. The eyes of all in the synagogue were fixed on him.
> Then he began to say to them, "Today this scripture has been fulfilled
> in your hearing." (Luke 4:16–21.)

All Things to All People...Read John 11:1–27

The Gospel of John is different. This becomes evident with its opening words—read John 1:1–5 where Jesus is referred to as the *logos* (Greek for "word") of God; as such, Jesus was with God at the moment of creation, and is God's eternal Word for all time. The gospel writer establishes a series of contrasts or dualities and conflicts. An important aspect of John is the series of "I am" sayings of Jesus: "I am the bread of life; the light of the world; the door for the sheep; the good shepherd; the resurrection and the life; the way, and the truth, and the life; and, the true vine." In the Hebrew Bible, the phrase "I am" is usually associated with God—emphasizing God's character. God is portrayed as healer, helper, savior, and keeper. In the Gospel of John, Jesus uses the phrase "I am" (Greek *ego eimi*) twenty-six times. The phrase connects Jesus with the God of the Hebrew Bible who discloses the divine name to Moses (see Exodus 3:13–15). The divinity of Jesus is rooted in God. The humanity of Jesus is rooted in the incarnation—God's Word made flesh. Jesus identifies himself by using the "I am" phrase: "Very truly, I tell you, before Abraham was, I am" (John 8:58). The Gospel of John begins with Jesus' heavenly origins rather than his earthly origins.

John 11 records the last signs of Jesus' earthly ministry. The resurrection of Lazarus is found only in John. Lazarus, Mary and Martha are good friends of Jesus; they live in Bethany, about two miles from Jerusalem where Jesus' opponents are waiting to arrest him. Against the better judgment of his disciples, Jesus goes to Bethany to see Lazarus' sisters who are mourning his death.

In John 11, Jesus and Martha have a theological discussion about death and resurrection. She believes that Jesus could have prevented her brother's death. She believes in a general resurrection on the last day of existence when God's judgment will be fulfilled. Jesus' declaration, "I am the resurrection and the life," is a statement of his power over death. Physical death is not ultimate—as "the life," Jesus offers everlasting life. The final reality is not death but Jesus. Those who believe in Jesus will live despite physical death—they will never die because Jesus is the way to an eternal relationship with God.

Why We Need this Story

When asked to share a Bible verse, some go to one of the shorter verses, "Jesus wept." (John 11:35.) This recitation sometimes brings a giggle or a look of exasperation from others who wanted to recite it. This episode shows us a poignant side of Jesus, a human side of him. Grief and loss evoke some of the deepest and rawest emotions in us. Weeping is an appropriate reaction, as Jesus demonstrates. We would not condemn Job for weeping and it's a pity that so many boys and men are admonished not to cry. I remember my father's attempt to "toughen up" my younger brother. Their conversation went like this:

> Father: "Listen, son. Big boys don't what?"
> Son: "Cry."
> Father: "Right! Now wipe those tears and don't let me see you cry again."

My brother couldn't have been more than three or four years old. My father was not a tyrant or a mean father, he did what he thought was best for his son in those days. Thank goodness that kind of thinking is changing—if God and Jesus can weep, surely men in our society can shed a tear. And let's be clear, there are things that warrant our tears; crying is a good thing!

Jesus is our faithful companion who had a range of human experiences that are like our own. He doesn't just show us the way, he leads the way.

Reflection Questions

1. What picture of Jesus emerges from this passage? Explain your answer.

2. What message is John conveying by including this story in his gospel?

3. What might death and resurrection mean from the perspectives of African Americans? Native Americans? Asian Americans? Hispanic Americans?

4. What in your life needs a resurrection and new life? How might resurrection happen for you?

Eleven

The Acts of the Apostles

After this, when Jesus knew that all was now finished, he said (in order to fulfill the scripture), "I am thirsty." A jar full of sour wine was standing there. So they put a sponge full of the wine on a branch of hyssop and held it to his mouth. When Jesus had received the wine, he said, "It is finished." Then he bowed his head and gave up his spirit.
(John 19:28–30.)

God Is Doing a New Thing...Read Acts 2:1–47

The Acts of the Apostles, a companion volume to Luke's Gospel, is more accurately about the beginnings of the Christian church. From the late second century CE, tradition establishes "Luke" as the author of both the Gospel of Luke and Acts. Luke is an anonymous writer, possibly a Greek-speaking convert to Judaism and later to Christianity. An apostle (in Greek, *apostolos*, "one who is sent out") is one specially commissioned to deliver a message or carry out some instruction on behalf of another. In the New Testament, the apostles are those who were part of Jesus' inner circle, especially the twelve disciples and the women who actually witnessed the work of Jesus and were beneficiaries of his teachings. Paul, who may have witnessed Jesus but was not part of the inner circle, has to work hard to convince others that he is also a true apostle. Both Peter and Paul are prominent apostles in Acts, but the book shows how others helped to establish the church.

The Book of Acts outlines the foundations of the Christian movement from Jerusalem to the outer reaches of the Roman Empire and the role of the Holy Spirit in the development of the church. Highlights of the book include the conversion of Paul to Christianity (see Acts 9) and the inclusion of Gentiles through the household of Cornelius (see Acts 10 and 11).

The Book of Acts focuses on a number of themes:

• The God of the Israelites is the same God who continues to work in history; the Christian movement is firmly rooted in the Judaic tradition.

• Jesus of Nazareth is God's Messiah who continues God's redemptive work on earth. The crucifixion and resurrection are seen as part of God's ongoing work to bring "Israel" into covenant community.

• All who repent and claim Jesus as Savior, Redeemer, Deliverer, will be saved whether Jew or Gentile. God's new world order is inclusive and available to all who wish to participate.

• Those who belong to Jesus (claim Jesus as Savior) will receive the gift of the Holy Spirit—who calls persons into community to be a prophetic witness to the power of God in the world.

• The Christian community lives in the expectation of Jesus' return and the universal restoration of God's "new Israel."

The return of Jesus is called the "Second Coming" or the Parousia (from a Greek word meaning "arrival," "coming," and "being present"). It is often connected with the judgment of God and is linked to the Hebrew Bible prophetic expectations. The Parousia is also linked to God's Reign in the preaching of John the Baptist and Jesus—both as signs that the present age has ended and God's new age has begun. During the "last days," there would be the last judgment and the resurrection of the dead. The delay of the Parousia was quite problematic for the early church. People found it hard to explain convincingly why Jesus had not yet returned. The challenge, then, was how the church should govern itself until Jesus' return. Today, the church continues to live in the expectation and hope that Jesus will return; however, the sense of urgency and the acuteness of the expectation have waned considerably.

The Book of Acts contains historical information but should not be considered history in the ways that we usually understand the term. Acts is the story of the early church told from the perspective of Luke—its purposes include showing how Christianity is rooted in Judaism; showing how Christianity is not at odds with the wider world; showing how God's new world order includes Jews and Gentiles united in community; and showing how the Holy Spirit worked to ensure the survival of the early church. The church's ongoing survival is tied to its connection to the Holy Spirit—an understanding that is often lost in some of our congregations. Part of this is because the Book of Acts is used so sparingly in the preaching and teaching of the church.

Our Bible study passage is the story of Pentecost. In Hebrew, Pentecost means "fiftieth day" and designates the fifty days that separate Pentecost from the Passover. Pentecost, also known as the Feast of Weeks, was one of three pilgrimage celebrations held in Jerusalem. Entire households were expected to gather to celebrate the blessings of God (see Exodus 23:16, Leviticus 23:15–21, Deuteronomy 16:9–12). The early church transformed a Jewish celebration into a Christian one.

Fifty days after the devastation of the crucifixion during Passover, the followers of Jesus celebrate the resurrection and the new life inaugurated by the coming of God's Holy Spirit. The Holy Spirit arrives with power and causes quite an uproar. It also provides an opportunity for Peter to preach a powerful sermon—this was no drunken folly; this was the fulfillment of Joel's prophecy (see Joel 2:28–32), when God would pour out God's Spirit on all flesh, men and women, who would have visions, dreams, and power; this event connected Jesus with the eternal dynasty of David and was proof that Jesus was resurrected by God to continue God's redemptive work on earth (Acts 2:14–36).

All those who witnessed the work of the Holy Spirit and heard Peter's sermon were convinced and asked Peter what should be done. And Peter does not disappoint—see Acts 2:38–39. Conversion to Christianity included repentance, baptism, forgiveness of sins, and the receiving of the Holy Spirit. The character of the early church community included fellowship, study, and the sharing of possessions.

Why We Need this Story

This passage is often used for evangelistic purposes or to chastise congregations that are more demure in their worship style. More quiet congregations are called "God's frozen people" and stand in stark contrast to the noisy, lively, chaotic Pentecost event in Acts 2.

This text also helps clarify the question of "speaking in tongues." The Acts text indicates that people were able to speak known languages although they had not been taught those languages—they suddenly became multilingual. This is not the same as glossolalia, or the "speaking in tongues"—

not human languages, but ecstatic utterances—of the sort described in 1 Corinthians 14, which Paul described as empowering the ministries of those who experienced it. But in the Acts narrative, Luke presents the speaking of multiple human languages as evidence of the Holy Spirit's anointing—undoing the Tower of Babel curse of linguistic separation and dissention, and allowing God's message to be preached to all.

In Luke's book of Acts, the outpouring of the Holy Spirit is a gift to the community, since all those gathered experienced it (see Acts 2:3–4). God's promised Spirit arrives with much fanfare and energy. The band of disappointed disciples and followers of Jesus are suddenly emboldened and empowered to embody the Jesus message and mission. The church is rooted and sustained by God's power through the Holy Spirit—just as Jesus had predicted. The household of God, gathered in Jerusalem to commemorate a Jewish celebratory feast, received the gift of God's Spirit—God continues to be faithful to God's people. This Spirit is poured out to unify and not divide God's people.

Reflection Questions

1. The Holy Spirit arrives and empowers the community of believers in Acts 2. Against this backdrop, how do you understand the statement, "Faith is personal, but not private"?

2. What image of the Holy Spirit emerges from this passage? Explain your answer.

3. How does the Holy Spirit work in the church and the world today? Explain your answer.

4. Given the character of the Christian community in Acts 2:43–47, what does the church need to do in order to recapture that vision?

Twelve

The Letters of the New Testament

*For I am not ashamed of the gospel; it is the power of God for salvation
to everyone who has faith, to the Jew first and also to the Greek.
For in it the righteousness of God is revealed through faith for faith;
as it is written, "The one who is righteous will live by faith."*
(Romans 1:16–17.)

Traditionally, Paul is thought to have written a large portion of the non-gospel materials in the New Testament. Biblical scholars now agree that Paul is not the author of all of the letters, or epistles, of the New Testament. The New Testament includes 21 letters divided into two general groups: those written by Paul (Romans through Philemon) and those not written by Paul (Hebrews through Jude). The collection of letters deals with the work and ministry of Paul as well as the leadership and organization of early Christian churches. The letters are arranged according to length—the longer letters appear first, which places the letters in a non-chronological order.

Letters are addressed to churches (Romans through 2 Thessalonians) and to individuals (1 Timothy through Philemon) and cover a wide range of concerns. They provide theological instruction, pastoral advice and care, and admonitions around morality and lifestyle. The letters highlight the spiritual challenges and theological controversies that confronted believers in an inhospitable setting. The "authors" of these letters are both pastors and teachers, not theologians in the contemporary sense of the word. Further, we have only one side of the conversation; that is, we don't know what the churches or individuals wrote that gave rise to the letters we have in the Bible. We can only guess at the events that occasioned them.

We know that the letters deal with real and concrete issues and concerns of people seeking a deeper faith and more committed discipleship. Paul traveled to cities as a missionary, starting new churches and supporting established ones. His message of God's grace was welcomed by the urban poor and powerless. The backdrop for Paul's work is Roman dominance and influence as well as the core traditions of Judaism, especially the teachings found in the Torah.

The non-Pauline letters were written by a diverse group of persons. The issues dealt with in these letters are more social than mission-oriented. The addressees are marginalized because of their faith and because their values are in conflict with the wider social context. They hoped for a new world order—one with socio-economic and political implications.

Paul is the church's first bona fide theologian—his important contribution is the inclusion of Gentiles into the faith. Remember that Jews in Jerusalem who felt connected to the Mosaic traditions of ancient Israel started the early Christian movement. Paul declared that Gentiles were included in the vision of a "new Israel," as the chosen people of God. Paul's missionary work took place in the urban centers of the Roman Empire and centered on the poor and marginalized. In this way, Paul continued the work of the Hebrew Bible's prophets who urged Israel to take up the concerns of the poor and oppressed.

Paul's letters followed a fairly firm pattern: an opening greeting; a statement of thanksgiving or prayer for the addressees; the main body which addresses some concrete concern or conflict in that congregation—this section might be mostly *kerygma* (theological teaching and instruction) or *paraenesis* (moral imperatives); a benediction which might also include further advice, greetings to specific individuals, personal news, a summary of the main body of the letter; and a doxology or prayer. The letter would end with a statement that served as his signature.

The Pauline Epistles (letters attributed to Paul) are difficult to place chronologically. A rough chronology is: 1 and 2 Thessalonians; Galatians; 1 Corinthians; Philippians; Philemon; 2 Corinthians; Romans; Colossians, and Ephesians.

Paul (also known as Saul; his name was changed after his conversion to Christianity) grew up in Tarsus of Cilicia; was a Roman citizen; was educated in Jerusalem; and was a member of the Pharisees. His early vocation focused on persecuting the followers of Jesus. He had a miraculous conversion experience and became a great preacher, missionary, and church planter for Christianity. Paul was firmly rooted in the Judaic traditions of Moses; at the same time, he was open to a multicultural vision of God's Reign.

As the Parousia (the Second Coming of Christ) was delayed, the early Christians lost their sense of urgency and settled into life by assimilating into the wider culture. Many of Jesus' and Paul's values and teachings were reversed as the people lost their fervor waiting for the fullness of God's Reign to be manifested. That is, the people fell back into the ways that they had abandoned with their initial conversion. The letters provide a glimpse, albeit a one-sided glimpse, into the life and struggles of early Christian communities as they tried to live faithful lives. The letters continue to serve a theological function by helping today's church remember its roots and by providing some strategies for dealing with conflict. The letters continue to inform, instruct, and inspire us.

Thirteen

The Pauline Letters

There is one body and one Spirit, just as you were called to the one hope of your calling, one Lord, one faith, one baptism, one God and [Parent] of all, who is above all and through all and in all. (Ephesians 4:4–6.)

Because of Christ, This is How We Live...
Read 1 Corinthians 13:1–13

Our Bible study passage is a familiar one—many people choose to include it in wedding ceremonies. It speaks of unselfish caring for another and certainly makes a good foundation for marriage and romantic commitments. However, Paul is not talking about romantic love here. Instead, Paul is talking about the affection and connection that is firmly rooted in God's care for humanity. For Paul, love is our response to God's gift to humanity and always points beyond humanity. God's love is manifested and embodied in Jesus Christ as the gift of salvation and redemption for humankind. God's love is the only ultimate and meaningful reality of this life. Love that is rooted in God allows us to love others—not because of what they can do for us, but because they, too, are God's people. Love finds its fulfillment in its connection to God and not just in another person.

Paul writes this treatise on love to a church that is struggling with its identity. Corinth had a reputation as a sinful city—its population was transient with diverse people moving in and out of the city; the wealthy did not care about the poor and used opportunities to oppress those who were marginalized. The church at Corinth grappled with concerns about morality and lifestyle issues, and with how to understand and rightly exercise spiritual gifts. The Christian community at Corinth often misunderstood Paul's teachings and tried to live both as citizens of the Roman Empire and as citizens of the "new Israel" of which Paul taught. There were numerous confusions and conflicts within the church at Corinth, including over whether the evidence of special gifts amounted to proof of their spirituality. Paul writes to them to re-focus their attention, and to remind them that the important thing is not what gifts they have and how they revel in those gifts. The important thing is that whatever gifts they possess, they have because of God's gracious act of salvation and love—not just affection, but love that is rooted and grounded in God's grace and compassion.

Why We Need this Story

This beautiful passage echoes Jesus' understanding of God's plan for creation; in Matthew 22:34–40, Jesus declares that the greatest commandments are to love God with our whole being and to love our neighbor as we love ourselves. All gifts—spiritual and otherwise—are useless if they don't spring from love for the sake of love.

Paul's lengthy list of love's characteristics requires a close reading and deep reflection—love and justice go hand in hand. We cannot have one without the other. Christianity has a spotty history when it comes to love—much good is done but there are a lot of mean-spirited deeds on the record, too.

If we were to take love seriously, as Paul challenges us to do, we could have a much better world. Instead, we violate God's intentions for community and then dare to ask where God is when the consequences manifest themselves. The love that Paul lifts up in 1 Corinthians 13 is rooted, grounded, and nurtured in and by God. It is permanent, complete, and supreme. Faith is wonderful, but sterile without love. Hope is life-giving but lonely without love. Love keeps faith and hope alive and makes everything else in life possible.

Reflection Questions

1. What picture of Paul emerges from this passage? How does he understand spiritual gifts?

2. How does Paul understand love?

3. To what question or concern is this passage an answer?

4. What hinders us in the twenty-first century from exhibiting the kind of love that Paul highlights here?

5. Write a definition of love—using this passage and your experiences of love.

▼ ▼ ▼

No, in all these things we are more than conquerors through him
who loved us. For I am convinced that neither death, nor life, nor angels,
nor rulers, nor things present, nor things to come,
nor powers, nor height, nor depth, nor anything else in all creation, will
be able to separate us from the love of God in
Christ Jesus our Lord. (Romans 8:37–39.)

Free at Last...Read Galatians 3:23-29

The Christian movement outside of Jerusalem drew large numbers of Gentiles. There were bound to be tensions, then, between those Jews who started the Christian movement and those non-Jews who joined the movement later. A major concern centered on whether one had to be a Jew in order to become Christian. In other words, did non-Jews have to observe the instructions of the Torah before they could profess faith in Jesus? There were Jewish-Christian teachers and missionaries who taught that, indeed, one had to be Jewish before one could be Christian. They advocated circumcision and observance of dietary regulations and other rituals of Judaism.

Paul stated, unequivocally, that observing the "law" was not necessary for one to be Christian. Galatians sets forth his argument in this matter. His argument is difficult to follow at points, but the bottom line is that Christ has set all persons free from the burden of trying to live up to the instructions of the Torah. The law was given to make persons aware of their transgressions and to define what constituted transgression and sin. The law makes one aware, too, that grace is needed. It is grace that God offers to all. Salvation through faith in Christ as God's ongoing work is available to all—even Gentiles! God has graciously provided another way to the divine. The cross marks the end of the old age and the beginning of a new age; the crucifixion opens a way for God's "new" creation and "new" Israel—an experience of Christ through the Holy Spirit is the only requirement. Paul emphasizes God's initiative in the salvation process and God's Spirit in the ongoing work of keeping persons in right relationship with God.

Galatians gives us a glimpse of the difficulties of merging the old with the new—Paul declares that God is radically inclusive and that all are invited to participate in God's plan and purpose for creation. The very presence of the Holy Spirit is proof that there is new life through Jesus Christ. He quotes Hebrew Bible passages to support his argument—see Genesis 15:6: Abraham received God's promise of blessing before he was circumcised and before the giving of the Torah through Moses! Further, the Abraham, Sarah, and Hagar story indicates God's inclusive promise—all before the events of Moses and the Torah. The Torah was a temporary measure designed to keep the people on track until God's new world order was fulfilled; for Paul, that fulfillment happened in the crucifixion and resurrection of Jesus.

Because of the Christ event, salvation is available for all who wish to participate. Christ eliminates separation and creates one people, one community, one family—where there is equality and unity. Note that in Galatians 3:28, the third element of Paul's groupings, male-female, is different from the first two. The first two set up a contrast: Jew *or* Greek, slave *or* free; but in the third, there is no longer male *and* female. This statement would have been a great shock for many of Paul's followers. There is a prayer that says it all—upon waking each morning, Jewish men thank God they were not slaves or women!

Scholars believe that Paul anticipates a world order where there is no more gender bias. It's not that men will no longer be men or women no longer women—it means that gender will not be a factor in how persons are treated and there will be no conflict between the genders. Some believe that Paul is quoting a baptism ritual that echoes the language and understanding of male and female at creation; see Genesis 1:27. Paul calls for egalitarian relationships that included women in strong leadership roles and active church participation.

Paul teaches that the Christ event is the continuation of God's work that began with Abraham. God intends to save the entire creation and that process has progressed in stages. For Paul, for the Galatians, and for all Christians, Jesus is the fulfillment of God's intention and purpose.

Why We Need this Story

The message of Galatians is one of inclusivity and would have been startling for early Christians. Remember that the Christian movement is solidly rooted in Judaism—Israel was God's Chosen People, set apart for a special purpose. Not just anybody could be Jewish; that is the message of the

Mosaic and Deuteronomic traditions. But now, the faith has been opened up and expanded. God's people now include those previously excluded—even Gentiles, even women! What's interesting to note is that Israel was always a diverse community. That diversity is simply carried over in God's new thing. God's grace reaches far and wide; the "law" was good back in the day. But God's grace has always been operative—even the giving of the law to Moses was an act of grace. Now, the act of faith in Christ places one within the range of God's care and household. God is doing a new thing by eliminating the barriers that separate people—nationality, ethnicity, social status, gender—all are one in Christ and constitute God's people. A new thing? Indeed! Good news? For sure!

Reflection Questions

1. What picture of Paul emerges from this passage? Explain your answer.

2. Who needs to hear the message of Galatians 3 today? Explain your answer.

3. Explain the importance of Galatians 3:23-29 for various communities of Christians today. What hinders the church from being fully inclusive?

4. What picture of God emerges in this passage?

Fourteen

The General Letters

I am reminded of your sincere faith, a faith that lived first in your grandmother Lois and your mother Eunice and now, I am sure, lives in you. For this reason I remind you to rekindle the gift of God that is within you through the laying on of my hands; for God did not give us a spirit of cowardice, but rather a spirit of power and of love and of self-discipline.
(2 Timothy 1:5–7.)

Who Can Be Called Faithful...Read Hebrews 11:1–12:2

The Letter to the Hebrews is not actually a letter; it is a sermon addressed to a mixed Greek-speaking community of Jewish and Gentile Christians. Scholars generally agree that Paul is not the book's author. The purpose of the book is to encourage its hearers to continue in their faith despite hardships and setbacks. The author connects Jesus to the Mosaic tradition of Israel. Jesus is the "high priest" who fulfills Jewish expectations for messianic salvation—now all have direct access to God. Listeners are encouraged to follow the example of Jesus by remaining faithful and patient even as they face persecution and oppression. The author draws upon traditions of Torah, Prophets, Psalms and Writings.

Our Bible study passage begins with a "definition of faith" (Hebrews 11:1) and outlines the life of faith by listing a number of personalities of the Hebrew Bible: Abel (see Genesis 4:4–10); Enoch (Genesis 5:24); Noah

(Genesis 6:8–9:17); Abraham (Genesis 12:1–8); Sarah (Genesis 17:19, 18:11–14, 21:2); Abraham and Isaac (Genesis 21:12, 22:1–10); Isaac (Genesis 27:27–40); Jacob (Genesis 48:8–22); Joseph (Genesis 50:24–25); Moses (Exodus 2:1–15, 12:1-28, 14:21–31); Rahab (Joshua 2:1–21, 6:12–21); Gideon (Judges 6–8); Barak (Judges 4–5); Samson (Judges 13–16); Jephthah (Judges 11–12); David (1 and 2 Samuel); and Samuel (1 Samuel 1–12).

These people on the "honor roll" of the faithful are not to be taken as role models; rather, they form the "cloud of witnesses" who maintained their faith under trying circumstances. There are a number of allusions to episodes in the Hebrew Bible. The bottom line of the book is that the believer must hold on to faith, no matter what. This chapter of Hebrews makes for great preaching if people know the biblical story. The author of Hebrews lists some colorful characters who often made foolish choices; yet their faith in God sustained them. Through their various trials, troubles, and tribulations, they understood that their hope and help resided in God. All of these, the faithful and fearless, never lived to see God's promises fulfilled; they all died before God's Messiah appeared. But Christ *has appeared* and is God's new thing and more than anyone could have imagined. What will we do with this marvelous opportunity?

Why We Need this Story

This long passage of scripture is powerful fodder for preaching and teaching. The references to characters in the Hebrew Bible carry stories, memories, and emotions guaranteed to move any congregation. The honor roll of the faithful highlights all manner of life situations—the horrors of slavery, the destruction of tsunamis and floods, the promise of fertility for a post-menopausal woman, the near slaughter of a youth at the hands of his father, the humiliation of being sold into slavery by one's jealous brothers, the wonder of being saved from massacre by floating in a basket on the River Nile, the prevalence of false arrests, violence, war, beatings, stonings, and persecutions. These and more surround us with the message that it's not over until it's over; or in the words of Joseph to his brothers:

> But Joseph said to them, "Do not be afraid! Am I in the place of God? Even though you intended to do harm to me, God intended it for good, in order to preserve a numerous people, as he is doing today. (Genesis 50:19–20.)

This cloud of witnesses in the Book of Hebrews continues to teach us what faith is: "the assurance of things hoped for, the conviction of things not seen." They teach us how to live in faith—enduring hardship, living in peace with each other, and trusting God!

Reflection Questions

1. Who should be added to the honor roll of the faithful? Why?

2. There are only two women (Sarah and Rahab) included in the honor roll of the faithful. Both are framed as stereotypes that make women's sexuality a commodity under the control of men. How might women find positive lessons from this passage?

3. Who today would find this passage affirming? In what ways is the passage affirming to you?

4. In what way is Jesus the ultimate example of faith? Explain your answer.

5. In what ways has your faith been tested? How did you overcome your trial, trouble or tribulation?

Rejoice in the Lord always; again I will say, Rejoice. Let your gentleness be known to everyone. The Lord is near. Do not worry about anything, but in everything by prayer and supplication with thanksgiving let your requests be made known to God. And the peace of God, which surpasses all understanding, will guard your hearts and your minds in Christ Jesus.
(Philippians 4:4–7.)

The Faith And Works Debate...Read James 2:14–26

The Letter of James is the first of the general or catholic letters; its placement does not mean it is the earliest of the non-Pauline letters. The author is unknown although tradition assigns it to James, a brother of Jesus. James writes to a Greek-speaking Jewish Christian community that is rooted in the ancient traditions of Israel. The purposes of the book include a reminder to keep God at the center of one's life; a declaration that one's faith and lifestyle should be in synch with each other; and an admonition that a life of faith demands acts of charity and compassion.

The community to which James writes is characterized by class distinctions (the wealthy oppress the poor) as well as unhealthy character traits like envy, greed, and violence. James warns them that such actions will be judged in the last days. In the meantime, Christians are called to live in harmony with each other and to work on behalf of the outcasts by engaging in concrete acts of service and charity.

The teachings of James are often seen as a contradiction to the teachings of Paul. A careful reading, though, reveals that James and Paul are on the same page with each other and with the teachings of Jesus. There is no separation between faith and acts of compassion and care. Jesus declared that the greatest commandments are to love God with one's whole self and to love one's neighbor as one loves self. James warns believers to practice what they preach and to walk the walk of faith—this always entails fulfilling social obligations within the community. Paul would not argue with James' imperative to be doers of the word. Certainly Jesus would have no argument!

Why We Need this Story

The book of James offers some practical guidelines for living a life of faith. He advocates perseverance in the face of adversity; in this, he echoes Job and the Psalmist. We walk *through* the valley of death, we don't stay there.

James warns us that riches and status are temporary and will fade away. He warns us to be careful about the words we use; words have the power to heal or to hurt. Christians should be intentional about speaking healing words. James tells us that we cannot control or manipulate the future—we do better by placing our hopes and trust in God. Patience, perseverance, and prayer mark the faithful life. James offers a lesson that is as timely today as it was in his day.

Reflection Questions

1. What picture of the ideal Christian church emerges from this passage?

2. In what ways is James speaking to you or your congregation about faith and works?

3. Rahab appears several times in the New Testament. How do you explain her inclusion in this passage?

Fifteen

The Apocalypse

In the beginning when God created the heavens and the earth, the earth was a formless void and darkness covered the face of the deep, while a wind from God swept over the face of the waters. Then God said, "Let there be light"; and there was light. And God saw that the light was good...
(Genesis 1:1–4a.)

The New Testament and the Protestant Bible closes with the Revelation **to John.** The Revelation is also known as the Apocalypse (in Greek, *apokalypsis*, meaning "revelation," "unveiling," "disclosure"). The apocalypse is an ancient literary genre traceable back at least to 250 BCE. The apocalypse is God's revelation about how the world will end; a seer or prophet describes visions of the end time. Although the book self-identifies as prophecy (see Revelation 1:3, 22:10), it fits the apocalyptic genre.

It is not clear who the author is. "John" knows and appreciates the workings of the Jerusalem Temple and the Hebrew Bible. Some scholars believe John was a Jewish Christian from Jerusalem who left Judah after the first Jewish Revolt against the Romans (66–73 CE). What is more certain is that the author was known by the seven Christian communities in the Roman province of Asia (see Revelation 1:9). The communities addressed represented a diverse cluster of churches dealing with issues of politics, economics, and religion. It is traditionally believed that the book was composed near the end of Domitian's rule, 81–96 CE.

Revelation is quite an odd book and has generated much discussion and disagreement about how to interpret it. There are strange visions, exaggerated language, bizarre images and symbolic uses of numbers, animals, angelic figures and such. It smacks more of science fiction and fantasy than religion. However, its themes are eternal: God is the ultimate authority for life and faith, and the challenge of the believer is to maintain faith in the midst of persecution and death. We have seen these themes lifted up throughout the biblical story.

The Book of Revelation creates difficulty for most Christians and for women in particular. There are a number of female images in this book; however, almost all of those images are detrimental for women. The "new Jerusalem" is depicted as a bride adorned for her husband (see Revelation 21:2) and implies "she" is a virgin. At the same time, Rome is depicted as a "Babylonian whore" (Revelation 17:4) and implies an uncontrollable entity. There is the vision of the woman, baby and dragon (see Revelation 12). These three examples effectively circumscribe women's roles in the first century society—virgin, mother, and whore. Each role connotes male control or lack of it. The message echoes the misinterpretation of Genesis 2–3 that portrays good women as obedient and pure while bad women are disobedient and unchaste.

The author frames the apocalypse in the form of letters to seven churches. Each church receives encouragement for faithfulness or chastising for disobedience. It is important to remember that the apocalypse as a literary type is designed to be over-the-top—it is impossible to "decode" the symbols and we are not to read it literally. Some take Revelation to mean that only 144,000 men will be saved at the end of time; that there will be lakes of fire; and that weird animals will direct traffic flow either to heaven or to hell. But that misuses the metaphors and symbols of apocalyptic imagery. The symbols and language of the Apocalypse are not self-evident; we must see them as symbols pointing to a reality—that God is in control of what happens at the end. The book of Revelation closes with the binding of the devil (Revelation 20:1–3), the resurrection and judgment (Revelation 20:11–15), and the inauguration of God's new heaven and new earth (Revelation 21:1–22:5). The message of the book is simple: those who persevere and remain faithful will be saved, regardless of how the world ends.

It is fitting that the Bible begins with creation and ends with the consummation of God's plan of judgment and salvation. In the beginning, God created the cosmos. In the end, God will judge and restore. We started our journey learning of God's creative process; we anticipate the end of our journey with the expectation of the fulfillment of God's creative vision.

"I am the Alpha and the Omega," says the Lord God, who is and who was and who is to come, the Almighty. (Revelation 1:8.)

God's New Thing, Revisited...Read Revelation 21:1–7

The Book of Genesis is about beginnings; the Book of Revelation is about endings. After John has visions about the glory of God, the opening of scrolls and seals, the sounding of trumpets, the praising of God, the executing of seven plagues, the coming victory of Christ and the heavenly armies, the binding of the Devil, and final judgment of the dead—John saw a new heaven and a new earth!

This Bible study passage reveals the transformation of creation—there will be a new heaven and a new earth (see Isaiah 65:17, 66:2). The new thing that God began at creation will finally be realized and fulfilled. It is important to note that the transformation is God's work. It is God's ongoing work in creation.

The author refers to several Hebrew Bible passages—see Isaiah 25:8, 35:10, 61:10 and Ezekiel 37:27. In verse 6, God discloses more of the divine character; God is "alpha and omega," the first last letters of the Greek alphabet. God is every thing, the beginning and the end and everything in between. And with this, we have come full circle—from beginning to ending. And God prevails!

Why We Need this Story

I love the book of Revelation! Surely you have guessed by now that I'm attracted to what is most quirky and problematic in the Bible. And nothing is as quirky and problematic as Revelation. It is almost impossible to get a handle on this book; the images are made for Hollywood—action, thrills, psychological conflict, explosions, chaos—it has everything for a blockbuster hit!

Despite the difficulties of interpretation, I love the bottom line of this book—those who remain faithful are to be rewarded with eternal life in God's new Jerusalem. Imagine a time and place where there will be no more sorrow, tears, pain, or death! Imagine a place with twelve gates—three on the north, three on the south, three on the east, and three on the west—so anyone and everyone can enter! Imagine a place so beautiful, we are almost blinded by its brilliance! Imagine basking all day and all night in God's presence! Imagine dining and talking with Jesus whenever we want! And to have all this, we have to remain faithful—so simple and so difficult. We have seen how hard it is to stay connected to God—but hope is alive. God is doing a new thing! Can you perceive it?

Reflection Questions

1. Have you been reluctant to study the Book of Revelation? Why or why not?

2. What is the significance of "Jerusalem" in the biblical story? What are the implications of a "new Jerusalem"? For whom is the "new Jerusalem" good news? For whom would it be bad news?

3. What does God mean in verse 6, "It is done!" What is "it"?

4. In what ways is God alpha and omega for you?

Sixteen

The Bible and the Church

So, here we are—we have looked at the Bible as a whole and in some of its parts. Christian community is rooted in God's love and creative process. We learn about the character and nature of God through the biblical witness of God's saving acts in history. From the stories of creation in Genesis to the new heaven and new earth of Revelation, the Bible tells us about God who loves us and invites us to participate in the divine creative process. The Bible is a witness to the Good News of Jesus Christ and the ongoing work of the Holy Spirit. The Bible is an important part of our identity and in the ongoing formation of our faith. We gather as a community to hear the stories of our faith, to worship the God we know as Creator, to celebrate the Jesus we know as Brother and Redeemer, and to receive the Holy Spirit we know as Sustainer and Comforter. The Bible helps us to know God and to know ourselves. Through word, sacrament, mission, and stewardship, we live out our faith and serve as witnesses to God's ongoing presence and work in the world.

Preaching and the Bible

God's people from the ancient days of Israel to the present time have gathered to remember God's presence and saving acts. Israel adapted the ancient feasts, festivals and rituals of its neighbors to reflect its understanding of the One God. Likewise, Christians have adapted Jewish celebrations to reflect our understanding of God's redemptive work through the person, ministry,

119

death and resurrection of Jesus of Nazareth. Preaching is the proclamation of the Christian message to the gathered faith community. We are assured that whenever two or three are gathered, Jesus is in the midst of them. Each week, we gather to hear God's Word. Many churches use the lectionary as a way of structuring their worship life.

A lectionary is a weekly schedule of biblical passages to be read and heard in the gathered community of Christians. Lectionaries include readings from the Hebrew Bible and the Christian Scriptures. They cite the biblical book, chapters and verses of the readings. Some lectionaries include information or suggestions for using the texts selected. Lectionary-based churches all hear the same scripture on any given Sunday—regardless of denomination or geographical location, Christians worldwide will focus on the same scriptures. The lectionary's purpose is to provide a way to read major sections of the Bible in an orderly fashion. The most widely used lectionary is the Revised Common Lectionary (RCL), used by both Catholics and Protestants. The schedule of readings include a passage from the Hebrew Bible, the Apocrypha (for Catholic circles), or the Acts of the Apostles; a passage from one of the psalms; another from either Revelation or the epistles; and a passage from one of the four gospels. The schedule of readings is a three-year cycle, with each year focusing on one of the Synoptic Gospels:

• Year A (Matthew) begins on the first Sunday of Advent in 2010, 2013, 2016, 2019, etc.

• Year B (Mark) begins on the first Sunday of Advent in 2008, 2011, 2014, 2017, etc.

• Year C (Luke) begins on the first Sunday of Advent in 2009, 2012, 2015, 2018, etc.

Only the Gospel of John lacks a year devoted to it. Parts of John are used at important points in the Christian year—Christmas, Lent and Easter.

The lectionary helps Christians move through the church year which begins with the first Sunday of Advent and moves through Christmas, Epiphany, Ash Wednesday, Lent, Palm Sunday, Maundy Thursday, Good Friday, Easter, Ascension Sunday, and Pentecost. The cycle then begins again. The lectionary is a tool to shape worship; there are times when preachers will want to preach from passages not listed in the lectionary. The lectionary, however, allows both preacher and laity to read and study the same passages and ensures that members will have a comprehensive understanding of the Bible and the church year.

Biblical preaching should attend to head, heart, and will—we should learn something as well as feel something and do something because of the sermons we preach and hear. This means paying attention to language and images. Inclusive language is not just about being "politically correct." It is also about living the radical inclusivity of God's vision for creation. Our words convey meaning and require our vigilant attention.

Worship and the Bible

The Bible is used in the liturgical life of churches through movement, song, prayer, and educational opportunities. Biblical passages form the foundation for prayers, calls to worship, rituals, sacramental elements, benedictions and the like. When Christians gather in worship, we are gathered around God's Word and we respond in joyful gratitude. The elements of worship and liturgy are not limited to the psalms, as one might suppose. The church has the challenge of celebrating the full message of God's saving deeds which means we must adapt the message and the expressions of the message for our contexts. Attention must be given to the language, and customs. Social settings must be taken into account as we shape worship.

Christian churches are communities of word and sacrament. We gather as God's people to confess our sins, to forgive one another and ourselves, to pray for others and for creation, to extend hospitality and peace, to hear God's Word and to celebrate God's presence in our midst. In addition to Sunday worship, we witness to and celebrate the baptism of those who accept God's invitation into God's household. We commemorate Christ's sacrifice at the communion meal; this is no empty ritual—it is a real meal with the risen Christ and is a foretaste of the heavenly banquet over which Christ will preside at the end of history. In the breaking of the bread and the sharing of the cup, we remember that we are one in the body of Christ, the church. We declare that all are welcome to the table.

Through our prayers, worship and sacraments, we rehearse God's gracious acts and celebrate God's love, grace, and mercy towards us.

Education and the Bible

In the development of Bible study and other educational opportunities, we want to get folks excited about the Bible. Church education should speak to the whole person—physically, spiritually, intellectually, and emotionally. There are a number of resources in the bibliography that will help you design programs and activities that take into account the different ways in which people learn. Don't be afraid to experiment—learning should be fun.

Educational programs should challenge folks to reflect on who we are as God's people and as God's community on earth. Bible study is a life-long enterprise and should be available at all stages of life and in a variety of settings. There is much in the Bible to inspire, encourage, and challenge us. Let us be open to the movement of the Holy Spirit as we continue our journeys toward wholeness—and the Bible can help!

Reflection Questions

1. What aspects of the biblical story are evident in your church's physical plant?

2. How do sermon and Bible connect in your church?

3. What acts of God are remembered in the sacraments of baptism and communion?

4. What is your church's plan for Christian education?

▼

Seventeen

A Closing Word

Well, we are done, my friends! We have journeyed through the Bible. And you are still breathing! You are still breathing, aren't you? I hope so—congratulate yourself for staying the course. You have done an amazing thing and I am proud of you—hooray!

I hope you had a good time traveling through the Bible. If you approached the Bible with fear and trembling, I hope you are now confident that you have a handle on the book we claim as scripture. And I hope that this is just the beginning of many more weeks and years of reading and studying the Bible—the sky is the limit because there is always something new and fresh in the Bible. And the Bible always calls us to something beyond where we are right now.

It still amazes me that I can bring my whole self to the Bible and have it speak to me, after decades of reading and studying. I am an African-American woman, born in the country and raised in the city by parents who were born in the middle of the Great Depression in rural Alabama. For the first ten years of my life, I was influenced by a diverse group of African-Americans on the south side of Chicago where family was important and everyone looked out for each other. All of my teachers were black and all were women until I entered fifth grade. Television was just gaining popularity in my youth, programming was limited and there were actually certain hours of the day when there was no programming—television actually went off the air between the hours of midnight and five a.m. or so. Further, as a child, I took for granted that stores and other businesses were closed on Sundays.

My favorite pastimes growing up were reading, listening to the stories of my parents, relatives and friends, and eavesdropping on the conversations of adults when they thought I was out of range. My family and I went to church sporadically—Easter, Christmas, Mother's Day, Father's Day, and whenever my grandparents visited! I grew up in a household where my father and mother took for granted that their children were college-bound. With the same assumptions on the part of my teachers, I never entertained any path other than that of higher education.

My teachers complemented my home training by exposing me to a world beyond my insulated neighborhood. But the world outside my small circle was not always kind. I encountered blatant incidences of racism and sexism. My parents and teachers did what they could to help me make sense of the world, but they couldn't always protect me.

The lessons of Jesus—turning the other cheek, loving my enemies, hanging in until God changed things—seemed awfully anemic in the face of the physical, verbal and psychological abuse and violence I saw on a regular basis. But when I was taught how to read the Bible, I realized that Jesus' teachings were subversive and liberating. Reading about Jesus in the Bible opened my eyes to a different set of possibilities—forgiveness is not about letting others off the hook, it's about my capacity to love deeply despite what others do. There have been times when my own mean-spirited and vengeful designs have been thwarted by some biblical incident or text—the Bible has kept me from degenerating to behavior like the one who was abusing, or attempting to abuse, me. My study of the Bible has given me courage, strength, and power to live as an African-American Christian woman—seeking to be a better person.

If the Bible can move me to do things I never imagined, just think what the Bible will do for you! Friends, we are part of a great adventure—God has made the way, Jesus leads the way, and the Holy Spirit pushes us along. We have everything we need for the journey—happy trails to you!

Final Reflection Questions

1. What surprised you most about studying the Bible?

2. What questions do you still have about the Bible?

3. At what points in the Bible did you find yourself? How did you respond?

4. What are the next steps for you in studying the Bible?

▼

Bibliography and Resources for Further Study

African American Heritage Hymnal. Chicago: Gia Publications, Inc., 2001.

Anderson, Bernhard W., *The Unfolding Drama of the Bible: Eight Studies Introducing the Bible as a Whole*. Philadelphia: Fortress Press, 1988.

Bañuelas, Arturo J. (ed.), *Mestizo Christianity: Theology from the Latino Perspective*. Maryknoll, NY: Orbis Books, 1995.

Blair, Christine Eaton, *The Art of Teaching the Bible: A Practical Guide for Adults*. Louisville: Geneva Press, 2001.

Blount, Brian (ed.), *True to Our Native Land: An African American New Testament Commentary*. Minneapolis: Fortress, 2007.

Borowski, Oded, *Daily Life in Biblical Times*. Atlanta: Society of Biblical Literature, 2003.

Bruce, Barbara, *Seven Ways of Teaching the Bible to Adults: Using Our Multiple Intelligences to Build Faith*. Nashville: Abingdon Press, 2000.

Brueggemann, Walter, *The Bible Makes Sense*. Louisville: Westminster John Knox Press, 2001.

———. *Hopeful Imagination: Prophetic Voices in Exile*. Philadelphia: Fortress Press, 1986.

———. *An Introduction to the Old Testament: The Canon and Christian Imagination*. Louisville: Westminster John Knox Press, 2003.

Cartlidge, David R. and David L. Dungan, *Documents for the Study of the Gospels.* Minneapolis: Fortress Press, 1994.

Countryman, L. William, *Interpreting the Truth: Changing the Paradigm of Biblical Studies.* Harrisburg: Trinity Press International, 2003.

Croatto, J. Severino, (trans. from the Spanish by Salvator Attanaiso), *Exodus: A Hermeneutics of Freedom.* Maryknoll, NY: Orbis Books, 1981.

Crossan, John Dominic, *Jesus: A Revolutionary Biography.* San Francisco: HarperSanFrancisco, 1994.

Day, Linda and Carolyn Pressler (eds.), *Engaging the Bible in a Gendered World: An Introduction to Feminist Biblical Interpretation in Honor of Katharine Doob Sakenfeld.* Louisville: Westminster John Knox Press, 2006.

Duck, Ruth C. (ed.), *Bread for the Journey: Resources for Worship.* New York: The Pilgrim Press, 1981.

Elizondo, Virgilio. *Galilean Journey: The Mexican-American Promise.* Maryknoll, NY: Orbis Books, 1983.

Essex, Barbara J., *Bad Boys of the Bible: Exploring Men of Questionable Virtue.* Cleveland: The Pilgrim Press, 2002.

——. *Bad Boys of the New Testament: Exploring Men of Questionable Virtue.* Cleveland: The Pilgrim Press, 2005.

——. *Bad Girls of the Bible: Exploring Women of Questionable Virtue.* Cleveland: The Pilgrim Press, 1999.

——. *Misbehavin' Monarchs: Exploring Biblical Rulers of Questionable Character.* Cleveland: The Pilgrim Press, 2006.

Felder, Cain Hope (ed.), *Stony the Road We Trod: African American Biblical Interpretation.* Minneapolis: Fortress Press, 1991.

Felder, Cain Hope, *Troubling Biblical Waters: Race, Class, and Family.* Maryknoll, NY: Orbis Books, 1989.

Gomes, Peter J., *The Good Book: Reading the Bible with Mind and Heart.* New York: Avon Books, 1996.

González, Justo L., *Mañana: Christian Theology from a Hispanic Perspective.* Nashville: Abingdon Press, 1990.

Gutierrez, Gustavo, (trans. from the Spanish by Matthew J. O'Connell), *On Job: God-Talk and the Suffering of the Innocent.* Maryknoll, NY: Orbis Books, 1987.

Haynes, Stephen R. and Steven L. McKenzie (eds.), *To Each Its Own Meaning: An Introduction to Biblical Criticisms and Their Application.* Louisville: Westminster/John Knox Press, 1993.

An Inclusive-Language Lectionary (three volumes). Atlanta: John Knox Press, 1986.

Isasi-Díaz, Ada María. "The Bible and Mujerista Theology." *Lift Every Voice: Constructing Theologies from the Underside.* Edited by Susan Brooks Thistlewaite and Mary Potter Engel. San Francisco: Harper & Row, 1990.

Kingsbury, Jack Dean, *Gospel Interpretation: Narrative-Critical and Social-Scientific Approaches.* Harrisburg, PA: Trinity Press International, 1997.

Malina, Bruce J., *The New Testament World: Insights from Cultural Anthropology.* Louisville: Westminster/John Knox Press, 1993.

Matsuoka, Fumitaka, *Out of Silence: Emerging Themes in Asian American Churches.* Cleveland: United Church Press, 1995.

Matthews, Victor H., *Old Testament Turning Points: The Narratives That Shaped a Nation.* Grand Rapids: Baker Academic, 2005.

McCary, P.K., *Black Bible Chronicles: Book One: From Genesis to the Promised Land.* New York: African American Family Press, 1993.

———. *Black Bible Chronicles: The Gospels—Rappin' with Jesus, The Good News According to the Four Brothers.* New York: African American Family Press, 1994.

Miller, Patrick (ed.), *Deep Memory, Exuberant Hope: Contested Truth in a Post-Christian World* by Walter Brueggemann. Minneapolis: Fortress Press, 2000.

Newman, Richard, *Go Down, Moses: A Celebration of the African-American Spiritual.* New York: Clarkson Potter, 1998.

Newsom, Carol A. and Sharon H. Ringe (eds.), *The Women's Bible Commentary.* Louisville: Westminster/John Knox Press, 1992.

Quinn-Miscall, Peter D., *Reading Isaiah: Poetry and Vision.* Louisville: Westminster John Knox Press, 2001.

Recinos, Harold J. *Hear the Cry! A Latino Pastor Challenges the Church.* Louisville: Westminster John Knox Press, 1989.

Sano, Roy (ed.), *The Theologies of Asian Americans and Pacific Peoples: A Reader.* Berkeley: Asian Center for Theology and Strategies, 1976.

Segovia, Fernando F. "Hispanic American Theology and the Bible: Effective Weapon and Faithful Ally." *We Are A People! Initiatives in Hispanic American Theology.* Edited by Roberto S. Goizueta. Minneapolis: Fortress Press, 1992.

Segovia, Fernando F. and Mary Ann Tolbert (eds.), *Reading from This Place: Social Location and Biblical Interpretation in the United States, Volume 1.* Minneapolis: Fortress Press, 1995.

Sugirtharajah, R. S. (ed.), *Voices from the Margins: Interpreting the Bible in the Third World.* Maryknoll: Orbis Books, 1995.

Takenaka, Masao, *God Is Rice: Asian Culture and Christian Faith.* Geneva, Switzerland: World Council of Churches, 1986.

Tinker, George E., *Missionary Conquest: The Gospel and Native American Genocide.* Minneapolis: Fortress Press, 1993.

Trible, Phyllis, *Rhetorical Criticism: Context, Method, and the Book of Jonah.* Minneapolis: Fortress Press, 1994.

Trible, Phyllis and Letty M. Russell (eds.), *Hagar, Sarah, and Their Children: Jewish, Christian, and Muslim Perspectives.* Louisville: Westminster John Knox Press, 2006.

Yee, Gale A. (ed.), *Judges and Method: New Approaches in Biblical Studies.* Minneapolis: Fortress Press, 1995.